Islam, Race and Being British
Contents

The Barrow Cadbury Trust

Established in 1920, the Barrow Cadbury Trust is a grant-making foundation that promotes social justice. We are committed to improving the situation of minority ethnic communities in the UK. In 1997, Barrow Cadbury was the principal funder of the seminal report on British Muslims and Islamophobia. We became involved as a result of our history of funding groups in the West Midlands. Our Inclusive Communities Programme supports Pakistani and Bangladeshi groups who are likely to be working with those facing the most severe disadvantage and discrimination.

Barrow Cadbury does not speak for the communities we support. Instead, we act as an intermediary between policy formers and those working at street level. We hope that our support helps grassroots groups engage with officials and enables them to develop opportunities within and around their communities.

Within the Inclusive Communities Programme, Barrow Cadbury has established "race and poverty" as a priority area of concern. We expect to identify work that promotes the further participation of Muslims in social, economic and political spheres. This will be complemented by initiatives that further promote understanding of the relationship between race, religion and national identity. However, our primary concern remains the disproportionate levels of unemployment, poor health and relative underachievement in education that are the lot of certain Muslim communities. We believe that greater emphasis on such basic, bread-and-butter issues is critical in overcoming the challenges that Muslims face.

Anna Southall, chair of the Barrow Cadbury Trust

Islam, Race and Being British

Edited by Madeleine Bunting

First published in 2005 by the Guardian in association with the Barrow Cadbury Trust.

The emergence of a Muslim identity politics © Tariq Modood
Is faith redefining the race equality project? © Paul Gilroy and Herman Ouseley
We've ditched race for religion © Safraz Manzoor
The challenge facing western Muslims © Tariq Ramadan
Can Islam make us British © Dilwar Hussain
How are we going to do God? © Sunder Katwala
Stop this folly now © Timothy Garton Ash
What kind of accommodation with Muslim demands is possible in a multicultural society? © Malieha Malik
Caught between two worlds; how can the state help young Muslims? © Shareefa Fulat
Negotiating new compromises © Geoff Mulgan
Questions of race and identity are clouding the more important issue of how to improve the everyday lives of British Muslims © Sukhvinder Stubbs
A community in crisis © Tahir Abbas and Phoebe Griffiths
England: a segregated country? © Ted Cantle
We have to be honest about the problems in the Muslim community © Ann Cryer
Attempts to anglicise Muslims will only backfire © Azhar Hussain
Interaction — where is it happening? © Indra Adnan
Who is talking to whom, and about what? © Farah Khan, Ehsan Masood and Asim Siddiqui
Habits of solidarity © Ash Amin

The Guardian is a registered trademark of the Guardian Media Group plc.

Printed in Great Britain by Masons Print Group
Text and cover design by the Guardian development department

ISBN: 0 85265 056 6

Preface

One of the founding principles of the Manchester Guardian when it was established in 1821 was religious freedom. In the early 19th century the Manchester reformers who founded the paper were concerned about the freedom of non-conformists to practise their beliefs: the Dissenters, Quakers and Congregationalists among others. Since 1821, the paper has applied this founding principle in different historical contexts.

Now, in 2005, this principle has a renewed significance given the prominence and intensity of the debate on the relationship between the west and Islam.

The urgency of this issue is twofold. We are daily witnessing the bloody global consequences of a perceived clash of civilisations — seen (rightly or wrongly) as a collision between Islamism and America's political and economic ambitions.

This international context is bearing heavily down on the UK's 1.6 million Muslims struggling to establish a secure British Muslim identity. The passage of anti-terror legislation has strengthened the sense of being under siege. It's a perception that finds fertile ground in a disproportionately young population which has grown up with chronically high levels of poverty and poor educational achievement.

The challenge is to develop new models of religious freedom in the 21st century that provide Britain's Muslim community with the kind of public recognition and affirmation needed, and which can be accommodated within British traditions. There are points of conflict — as this collection makes clear — and it is in places such as the Guardian that these can be worked through and new possible accommodations be explored.

This book is the fruit of a year-long collaboration with Barrow Cadbury to explore these critical debates and to open them up to a new, younger generation of participants within the Muslim community.

The enthusiastic response and commitment to the debate has been striking and I'm delighted that the Guardian will continue to run the Guardian Muslim Youth Forum on an annual basis so that the hard work of argument and debate — which is at the heart of a democratic, civic culture — will go on.

Alan Rusbridger, editor of the Guardian

Comment after the London bombings of 7/7
Orphans of Islam: Madeleine Bunting

The bombings in London on 7/7 were shocking enough but what has thrown British multiculturalism into an unprecedented crisis was the news that the four suicide bombers were all British-born Muslims. Three were of Pakistani background from a Leeds suburb and the fourth was a convert to Islam. As the details of these individuals' lives emerged, the sense of stunned disbelief has only deepened; they did not fit the stereotypes of alienated and dispossessed youth. These were individuals who had successfully integrated into British society in many important ways: one was at university, another was a much respected community volunteer working with young people and working in the local primary school as a learning mentor. Several had loving, close families and had children of their own. What these suicide bombers typified was not the failure of Muslim participation in British life, but its success. The challenge to our understanding of how to build a harmonious multicultural society has been shaken to the core.

What has followed has been the most frenzied scrutiny ever of the British Muslim community and how it has developed within multicultural Britain. Has the community been too introverted? Who are its leaders? Are they out of touch? Who do they represent? Who runs the mosques and what are they teaching their young? How is it that no one in the community was aware of what these four youngsters — the youngest was only 18 — were planning?

In the desperate desire for greater understanding of the atrocity of so many murdered lives in London, every aspect of the Pakistani British community in the northern towns such as Leeds and Dewsbury has been examined by the media. Key issues have emerged more clearly, such as the almost unbridgeable generation gap between the elders who run the mosques and the third generation. A generation of boys have grown up disorientated about their own sense of identity, their heritage and how they find a secure position in British society. As one Arab told the journalist Navid Akhtar in the early 90s, these were "orphans of Islam" and the extremists knew they had a constituency here.

One of the questions that will have to be confronted is whether the model of community leadership among British Muslims has been effective. How was it responding to the generation gap? Has it identified the correct issues on which to campaign? Has the interface with government been too focused on symbolic issues? Has it been sufficiently aware of the problems faced by a younger generation in less affluent parts of the country? The riots in the northern towns were a warning of the unease there; has enough been done to build the strong grassroots organisations required to tackle it?

It has been a painful time to be a British Muslim. On the one hand, the community has been subjected to a barrage of questions from the media, and on the other hand, a passionate debate of self-questioning has opened up within the community. At one meeting of young Muslims in

> 'What these suicide bombers typified was not the failure of Muslim participation in British life, but its success'

London 10 days after the bombing, there was a profound sense of failure: why has our community failed to transmit its Islamic values? Why has the Islamic tradition failed so many of its young in this country?

The reverberations of these events will be evident for months and years to come. It will impact on many aspects of life for British Muslims. Already, the police have warned that there will be an increase in stop-and-searches on Muslims; already the government has announced new anti-terror measures to combat the threat of more suicide bombings. Muslims will have to confront a greater degree of suspicion than ever before.

At the same time, within only a week of the bombings a new theme was emerging in the public reaction to the bombings: "force them to be ordinary" was the line taken up by one prominent commentator who urged that the introverted Muslim communities which could harbour such extremism had to be smashed open. Others might use gentler language but the response will be much the same and it will charge with new emotive force the debate around integration. The issues taken up in part three of this book around housing, education and communal traditions of intercontinental marriages will move centre stage. That debate already shows signs of being misplaced: the suicide bombers were in many ways, integrated.

But the underlying force of this argument will probably be unarguable and can be summed up as: non-Muslim Britain needs to understand British Muslims much better and needs to know them better if there is to be any hope of trust being rebuilt. All around us there are prophecies of doom — of more suicide bombers and spiralling distrust — so it's important to keep in mind that 9/11 was, among many things, a huge stimulus to the search for greater understanding of Islam. This London atrocity could play the same role; it is the kind of crisis that can bring about change in people's attitudes. It could help open up communities that have been introverted; it could prompt that very British character-istic of indifference into taking more interest in their neighbours. Amid all the gloom, it's important to point out that most Britons immediately distinguished between a small handful of extremists and the vast major-ity of British Muslims; to date, there has been no widespread violent per-secution and harassment of British Muslims.

This book had gone to press only days before the bombings. Many of the discussions that led to the articles in this book were in a context when the issues were less fraught and urgent. We no longer have that luxury; the London bombings hugely increase the importance of the challenges ahead of finding a secure and self-confident British Muslim identity. It is a hugely complex task: it ranges from the abstract intellec-tual work of mapping a concept of citizenship, such as that laid out by Tariq Modood, to the exploration of Islamic thought around being part of a minority community in a non-Muslim society and to the basic issues of community development and youth work. As Ajmal Masroor, one of the participants to the Guardian Muslim Youth Forum, makes clear below in his comment on the bombings, the task of developing new narratives of belonging is more pressing than ever. To face these challenges effec-tively requires much greater and more detailed knowledge and it requires a broad-based and searching debate in civil society. The hunger to understand, and the desire to find a distinctively British way through the complex challenges ahead make this book more timely than ever.
July 17 2005

Comment after the London bombings of 7/7

Ajmal Masroor

The recent London bombings have brought the debate into sharp focus for the Muslim community as Muslims and non-Muslims all ask the same question: "What went wrong?" Muslim theologians need to state very clearly and authoritatively what is and what is not acceptable; what is the appropriate response to the global grievances Muslims harbour about Iraq, Afghanistan and Palestine; and, most importantly, what makes someone a true Muslim. There is a common acceptance that anyone who performs the rituals, such as five daily prayers, fasting and pilgrimage, is a devout Muslim. Islamic scholars must answer whether ritual and dogma form the most important feature of Islam, and where moral and social responsibilities fit in.

I am very afraid of what will happen to us Muslims now. I wonder if we can find a big enough hole to hide in. How can I show my face to my neighbours when the London bombers are known to be Muslims? Will my wife in a hijab be safe on the streets of London? Would my elderly father be able to go the mosque as freely as he has done all his life? I can feel a great fear within the community. Many Muslims are staying at home, scared of being attacked. On the streets I notice people look at me differently: is he or is he not...?

So far we have had wishy-washy answers from our leaders, politicians and communities. British Muslims have a problem: why has the Muslim community failed to rein in their own youth and help them shape their future? Why have mosques failed to provide leadership, direction and vision to the community? Muslim leadership has never been so rigorously questioned; they are facing the biggest challenge from Muslim youth and from the non-Muslim community. Why have we failed? What about the old guards from the Muslim community who have perpetuated insularity and haven't been accountable as leaders? What about the undemocratic mosque committees? These are some of the questions that Muslim leaders need to clearly answer. We need to acknowledge our failure if we are to have any hope in the future.

At the same time, we have to ask, why has the government failed to recognise the strength of anger that Muslims feel about British foreign policy? Why is the government in denial? Palestine to Kashmir and Afghanistan to Iraq are all on fire. Who is responsible for this? Why have the politicians failed to deal with it adequately? They need to acknowledge their failure. We need people to take the politicians to task, and to demonstrate the people's democratic power to counteract the failed, misguided policies of our elected politicians. It is because of their misguided foreign policies that people are dying on the streets of London, Iraq and Palestine.

Furthermore, non-Muslims have failed to understand that they have not been open and welcoming of Muslims as part of the European identity — "we will tolerate you only" has been the message. I don't want you merely to tolerate me, I would like you to accept me for who I am. I

> 'People need to demonstrate their democratic power to counteract the failed, misguided policies of our elected politicians'

would like you to make space for me so that I can be part of a shared vision for the future; Muslims and non-Muslims: we all need to be equal partners in this debate about what kind of British society we want.

I feel alienated from your history, from your values, and from your experience. There is no shared paradigm, no shared heritage and certainly there is no room for developing a new narrative.

The media only focuses on Muslims when there is a problem. I have been questioned since 7/7 by the media at length about what I think; but what about the previous 30 years when the media didn't want to know? I also had views and I also played my part in society then, so why now is there so much interest? Islam and Muslims have been subject of intense interest but for the wrong reasons.

There has been a joint failure: I could be living in a neighbourhood and know nothing about my neighbours, and my neighbours would know nothing about me. It is unfortunate that it has taken bombs in London to awaken us to this debate. What we need now is a narrative around a hybrid identity, a new narrative — that is the future.

July 17 2005

Introduction
Madeleine Bunting

In January 2005, the Guardian and Barrow Cadbury launched an initiative, a simple idea with a big ambition. We pulled 50 people together for 24 hours and gave them two questions to thrash out. What are the consequences of an increasingly assertive Muslim political identity in Britain? If multiculturalism has been discredited, as Trevor Phillips claimed in 2004, what do you put in its place?

What resulted was an intense, passionate, sometimes fractious and thankfully, occasionally humorous, debate which sprawled from abstract argument about identity to concrete issues of how unemployment among Birmingham's Muslims is three times the city average and, how in some British cities, school playground fences separate ethnic groups so sharply it cannot but suggest comparison with apartheid. This book reflects this debate, giving space to the reflections of several participants and reprinting key contributions to this debate which have appeared on the Guardian's comment pages.

Neither this book nor the conference have produced a shopping list of clear-cut answers, but perhaps they will kick-start a much-needed debate and bring right out into the open the issue of how does the left — with its deeply secular instincts — deal with the reassertion of religion in British political life? This conundrum has split the left in a way that race issues have not done for several decades; all the left's inclinations are to insist that religion is strictly a private matter, but that is being profoundly challenged by a British Muslim community that uses many of the arguments and terms of identity politics developed around race and feminism with which the left has had such a close association for the last 30 years. For the left, two cherished principles are in conflict: its commitment to secular politics and its commitment to racial justice.

'What will be the left's response as British Asians increasingly choose to define themselves by their religion not their ethnicity?'

The result is a profound confusion and a real danger that the engine of British multiculturalism, the left, could falter at the very point when its vitality is most needed to accommodate a new challenge of diversity — a diversity of values rather than the diversity of ethnicity. This is an increasingly important political territory open to mobilisation and unscrupulous manipulation as a resource for new and destructive forms of national identity politics. This is a politics that revolves around questions of culture and values to define who is "one of us" and follows "our way of life". As one Muslim woman participant summed it up: "Am I only British when I get my suit from Next?"

If multiculturalism was the left's response to mass immigration in the 60s, slowly developed, patchily applied, frequently misunderstood but for all that, relatively successful, what will be the left's response to faith identities as British Asians increasingly choose to define themselves by their religion not their ethnicity? Multiculturalism has, to some extent, succeeded in dismantling the definition of British as white. Now another chapter has to be written in which British identity is no longer synonymous with a Christian/secular accommodation. Or put it another way, can Britain become more Muslim?

The first section of this book reflects these questions and how identity is being reconfigured. Tariq Modood, in his crucial essay, outlines the points of continuity between earlier forms of identity politics on race and gender and traces how the concepts they propagated of the private as political are being used by British Muslims in their quest now for recognition and accommodation.

If one has both a religious and a political identity, do they reinforce or undermine each other? The answer depends, of course, on how those two identities are defined; an Islamist reading of what it is to be a Muslim is not going to bed down easily with British democratic politics, nor will British identity as essentially Christian/secular be accessible to Muslims. These are the questions taken up by two Muslim thinkers in this section: Tariq Ramadan highlights some key issues, while Dilwar Hussain explores in more detail how Islamic teaching can inform a British citizenship.

The second section of the book looks at how the abstract issues of identity are expressed in politics. What kind of accommodation and recognition is required in the public sphere to affirm private identities and give them the sense of security required for belonging? What part can religion play in political life — what part does it already play in Britain? How then do we imagine — because all human communities are products first and foremost of the imagination — this national community which can offer more recognition and space to religious identities?

For many Muslims, the answers to these questions are still not clear and certainly not agreed. Some passionately want more Muslim state schools, others argue that they are an unwelcome form of segregation and that Muslims should seek common, equal citizenship. Some want sharia — Islamic family law — others are nervous of the cost to the rights of women, as Malieha Malik points out.

The parameters of faith in the public sphere are not resolved for any faith in the UK which, despite being a largely secular country, still pragmatically accommodates an established church and a head of state who is the head of a Christian church. But as Sunder Katwala details, old settlements are being challenged.

One participant to the conference prefaced her remarks with the statement, "I believe in God". You could hear, in the quality of silence in the room, the shock that religious belief is unapologetically trespassing into mainstream debate for the first time in over a generation. And it is triggering profound anxiety on the secular left, as both Timothy Garton Ash and Polly Toynbee express. The fear is that old struggles such as gay rights or feminism could be vulnerable to reversal and that old freedoms such as freedom of speech could also be vulnerable to attrition.

And always the international context hovers over these domestic discussions. It fires the fear with a particular intensity as fundamentalism emerges as an aberrant, aggressive phenomenon in all the world's religions — as militant Islamism finds its mirror image in militaristic evangelical Christianity — and the capacity for violence, for destruction of even long-standing co-existing communities, is increasingly evident. That could have painful reverberations in Britain. We only have to look at how the murder of the Dutch film-maker Theo Van Gogh has shaken confidence in the Netherlands' tradition of multiculturalism to see how fragile past accommodations can prove. Geoff Mulgan concludes this section by offering three lessons from history on how new deals can be negotiated.

The third section of the book shifts tack to look at the much more concrete issues of poverty and social exclusion. Sixty-nine per cent of all Pakistani and Bangladeshi children live in poverty. Yet the politicisation of the community, as Sukhvinder Stubbs points out, has been around the symbolic issues of public recognition such as legislation on incitement to religious hatred rather than on poverty. Kashmir and Iraq feature higher in the Muslim community's political agenda than child poverty and poor housing.

One of the most disturbing and challenging realities is the sheer visibility of the segregation of many urban neighbourhoods. The playground with a fence separating white from Muslim children is one example, and it is one found in many areas of the UK. Educational segregation is now more pronounced than residential segregation. This is where the questions about identity translate into the detail of individual lives: where and to whom do you belong? Whom do you know as friends and neighbours? Whom do you marry? Where are the connections and relationships which make your neighbourhood work or, if it's riddled with crime, suspicion and fear, where should they be? The vexed issue of segregation and integration was the one which kept bobbing to the surface during the conference — segregation is a "choice", "it's wrong"; integration, like broccoli, is good for you.

Ann Cryer and Azhar Hussain both argue for very different ways of living together in the town of Keighley. Many find it hard to accept a new pattern of migration which, unlike previous waves, has no desire for assimilation. Easy travel and communication enable strong hybrid identities in a way not possible in the past. One can live in Keighley and still play a vital role in the family's affairs back in Pakistan. The strength of that hybrid identity may mean that for Keighley families the model they want is interaction with the white community around them rather than integration which they associate with the diminution of their Pakistani heritage.

So when and who decides that some levels of segregation are detrimental to the common good, such as the increasing white flight from British cities, or introverted faith communities? We all live segregated lives to differing degrees; the English middle classes call it PLUs, People Like Us, and no one has demanded they do more to integrate. But compound segregation with chronic poverty, and it seems self-evidently dangerous, as the riots in the northern towns in 2001 proved. For the left, with its traditional preoccupation with solidarity, the questions of how to build bridges between communities, and of how and when the state should intervene — in school admissions, in housing allocations — are compelling. The left's belief that the state should provide equal life chances gives it an imperative to intervene — even to socially engineer — some forms of integration, as Indra Adnan explores in the government's social cohesion agenda.

One of the most common conclusions about many of the most contentious issues raised in these pieces is that they "need more debate". But where do the debates happen and who participates in them? In particular, what are the debates within the Muslim community, and what kind of debates are there between Muslim and non-Muslim? Three Muslims comment on their experiences of dialogue and debate, before Ash Amin concludes the section with his analysis of the challenge ahead.

Finally in the addendum we reprint the Guardian's supplement reporting on an unprecedented event in November 2004 when we invited 103 young Muslims and gave them the platform to discuss their view of a range of questions, from British foreign policy to the role of women. Here was the new voice of a new generation which is rarely given space.

Many of the issues raised in these pieces are so difficult that many on the left nervously retreat behind platitudes, giving dangerous quarter to the far right to distort perceptions, and fuel hatred. They run the risk of leaving the task of shaping public debate and imagining communities to those with less careful consciences and less goodwill. We can't afford to let them do so. The challenge is to develop habits of solidarity, both personal and political, despite differences of identity and values: habits of solidarity, from the smallest details of daily life, such as the civility of street transactions, to the big picture of a generously resourced educational system and the determination to tackle discrimination.

June 2005

Biographies

Tahir Abbas is director of the Centre for the Study of Ethnicity and Culture, University of Birmingham

Indra Adnan is director of the New Integrity consultancy

Ash Amin is professor of geography at the University of Durham

Madeleine Bunting is a columnist and associate editor on the Guardian

Ted Cantle CBE is associate director at the Improvement and Development Agency for Local Government; he chaired the review in 2001 into disturbances in the northern towns

Ann Cryer is the member of parliament for Keighley, West Yorkshire

Jonathan Freedland is a columnist on the Guardian

Shareefa Fulat is director of the Muslim Youth Helpline

Timothy Garton Ash is professor of European studies, Oxford, and a columnist on the Guardian

Paul Gilroy is author of After Empire: Melancholia or Convivial Culture, and professor of African American studies at Yale University

Phoebe Griffith is senior development manager at the Barrow Cadbury Trust

Azhar Hussain is a lecturer in accountancy for BPP in Leeds; he is one of the founders of Abu Zahra Foundation (www.abuzahra.org) and the Learning Zone in Keighley

Dilwar Hussain is a research fellow at the Islamic Foundation, Leicester

Sunder Katwala is the general secretary of the Fabian Society

Farah Khan is a freelance journalist and broadcaster; she is on the Regional Council of Arts Council England, North East

Malieha Malik is a lecturer in law at King's College, London

Safraz Manzoor is a broadcaster and Guardian columnist

Ehsan Masood is a freelance journalist

Ajmal Masroor leads Friday prayers in various London mosques and is a cultural relations consultant

Seumas Milne is comment editor of the Guardian

Tariq Modood MBE is professor of sociology, politics and public policy and the founding director of the Centre for the Study of Ethnicity and Citizenship at the University of Bristol; his most recent book is Multicultural Politics

Geoff Mulgan is director of the Young Foundation and former head of the Strategy Unit at No 10 Downing Street

Herman Ouseley is former chair of the Commission for Racial Equality, and author of the Community Pride Not Prejudice report into race relations in Bradford in 2001

Tariq Ramadan is the author of several books on Islam

Asim Siddiqui is an accountant; he is one of the founders of the City Circle (www.citycircle.org)

Sukhvinder Stubbs is chief executive of the Barrow Cadbury Trust

Polly Toynbee is a columnist on the Guardian

Gary Younge is a columnist on the Guardian

Part 1
What am I?
The politics of identity

The emergence of a Muslim identity politics

Tariq Modood

There is an anti-Muslim wind blowing across the European continent. One factor is a perception that Muslims are making politically exceptional, culturally unreasonable or theologically alien demands upon European states. My contention is that the claims Muslims are making in fact parallel comparable arguments about gender or ethnic equality. Seeing the issue in that context shows how European and contemporary is the logic of mainstream Muslim identity politics.

The British experience of "coloured immigration" has been seen as an Atlantocentric legacy of the slave trade, and policy and legislation were formed in the 1960s in the shadow of the US civil rights movement, black power discourse and the inner-city riots in Detroit, Watts and elsewhere. It was, therefore, dominated by the idea of "race", more specifically by the idea of a black-white dualism. It was also shaped by the imperial legacy, one aspect of which was that all colonials and citizens of the Commonwealth were "subjects of the crown". As such they had rights of entry into the UK and entitlement to all the benefits enjoyed by Britons, from NHS treatment to social security and the vote. (The right of entry, of course, was successively curtailed from 1962.)

The relation between Muslims and the wider British society and British state has to be seen in terms of the developing agendas of racial equality and multiculturalism. Muslims have become central to these agendas even while they have contested important aspects, especially the primacy of racial identities, narrow definitions of racism and equality, and the secular bias of the discourse and policies of multiculturalism. While there are now emergent Muslim discourses of equality and of difference, they have to be understood as appropriations of discourses whose provenance lies in anti-racism and feminism.

While one result of this is to throw advocates of multiculturalism into theoretical and practical disarray, another is to stimulate accusations of cultural separatism and revive a discourse of "integration". While we should not ignore the critics of Muslim activism, we need to recognise that at least some of the latter is a politics of "catching up" with racial equality and feminism. In this way, religion in Britain is assuming a renewed political importance. After a long period of hegemony, political secularism can no longer be taken for granted and is having to answer its critics; there is a growing understanding that the incorporation of Muslims has become the most important challenge of egalitarian multiculturalism.

> 'We have to recognise that some of Muslim activism is a politics of catching up with racial equality and feminism'

British equality movements

Muslim assertiveness became a feature of majority–minority relations only from around the early 1990s; indeed, prior to this, racial equality discourse and politics were dominated by the idea that the dominant post-immigration issue was "colour racism". One consequence of this is that the legal and policy framework still reflects the conceptualisation and priorities of racial dualism.

Till recently it was lawful to discriminate against Muslims *qua* Muslims because the courts did not accept that Muslims were an ethnic group (though oddly, Jews and Sikhs were recognised as ethnic groups within the meaning of the law). While initially unremarked upon, this exclusive focus on race and ethnicity, and the exclusion of Muslims but not Jews and Sikhs, came to be a source of resentment. Muslims do enjoy some limited indirect legal protection *qua* members of ethnic groups such as Pakistanis or Arabs. Over time, groups such as Pakistanis have become an active constituency within British "race relations", whereas Middle Easterners tend to classify themselves as "white", as in the 1991 census, and on the whole were not prominent in political activism of this sort, nor in domestic politics generally. One of the effects of this politics was to highlight race.

A key indicator of racial discrimination and inequality has been numerical under-representation, for instance in prestigious jobs and public office. Hence, people have had to be (self-)classified and counted; thus group labels, and arguments about which labels are authentic, have become a common feature of certain political discourses. Over the years, it has also become apparent through these inequality measures that it is Asian Muslims and not, as expected, African Caribbeans, who have emerged as the most disadvantaged and poorest groups in the country. To many Muslim activists, the misplacing of Muslims into "race" categories and the belatedness with which the severe disadvantages of the Pakistanis and Bangladeshis have come to be recognised mean that race relations are perceived at best as an inappropriate policy niche for Muslims, and at worst as a conspiracy to prevent the emergence of a specifically Muslim identity. To see how such thinking has emerged we need briefly to consider the career of the concept of "racial equality".

The initial development of anti-racism in Britain was directly influenced by American personalities and events. It was part of a wider sociopolitical climate which was not confined to race and culture or non-white minorities. Feminism, gay pride, Québecois nationalism and the revival of a Scottish identity are some prominent examples of these new identity movements which have become an important feature in many countries. Political theorist Iris Young describes the emergence of an ideal of equality based not just on allowing excluded groups to assimilate and live by the norms of dominant groups, but on the view that "a positive self-definition of group difference is in fact more liberatory".

Equality and the erosion of the public–private distinction

This significant shift takes us from an understanding of "equality" in terms of individualism and cultural assimilation to a politics of recognition; the latter involves a concept of equality that does not require one to hide or apologise for one's origins, family or community, and requires others to show respect for them. Public attitudes and arrangements must adapt so that this heritage is encouraged, not contemptuously expected to wither away.

These two conceptions of equality may be stated as follows:
● the right to assimilate to the majority/dominant culture in the public sphere, with toleration of "difference" in the private sphere;
● the right to have one's "difference" (minority ethnicity, etc) recognised and supported in both the public and the private spheres.

While the former represents a classical liberal response to "difference", the latter is the "take" of the new identity politics. The two are not, however, alternative conceptions of equality in the sense that to hold one, the other must be rejected. Multiculturalism, properly construed, requires support for both conceptions. For the assumption behind the first is that participation in the public or national culture is necessary for the effective exercise of citizenship, the only obstacle to which are the exclusionary processes preventing gradual assimilation. The second conception, too, assumes that groups excluded from the national culture have their citizenship diminished as a result, and sees the remedy not in rejecting the right to assimilate, but in adding the right to widen and adapt the national culture, and the public and media symbols of national membership, to include the relevant minority ethnicities.

It can be seen, then, that the public–private distinction is crucial to the contemporary discussion of equal citizenship, and particularly to the challenge to an earlier liberal position. It is in this political and intellectual climate — namely, a climate in which what would earlier have been called "private" matters had become sources of equality struggles — that Muslim assertiveness emerged as a domestic political phenomenon. In this respect, the advances achieved by anti-racism and feminism (with its slogan "the personal is the political") acted as benchmarks for later political group entrants, such as Muslims. As I will show, while Muslims raise distinctive concerns, the logic of their demands often mirrors those of other equality-seeking groups.

Religious equality

So, one of the current conceptions of equality is a difference-affirming equality, with related notions of respect, recognition and identity — in short, what I understand by political multiculturalism. What kinds of specific policy demands, then, are being made by or on behalf of religious groups, and Muslim identity politics in particular, when these terms are deployed? I suggest that these demands have three dimensions, which get progressively "thicker" — and less acceptable to radical secularists.

No religious discrimination: The very basic demand is that religious people, no less than people defined by "race"' or gender, should not suffer discrimination in job and other opportunities. So, for example, a person who is trying to dress in accordance with their religion or who projects a religious identity (such as a Muslim woman wearing a headscarf, a hijab), should not be discriminated against in employment. Till the end of 2003 there was no legal ban on such discrimination in Britain. This is, however, only a partial "catching-up" with the existing anti-discrimination provisions in relation to race and gender. It does not extend to discrimination in provision of goods and services, nor creates a duty upon employers to take steps to promote equality of opportunity.

Even-handedness in relation to native religions: Many minority faith advocates interpret equality to mean that minority religions should get at least some of the support from the state that longer-established religions do. Muslims have led the way on this argument, and have made two particular issues politically contentious: the state funding of schools and the law of blasphemy. The government has agreed in recent years to fund a few Muslim schools, as well as a Sikh and a Seventh Day Adventist school, on the same basis enjoyed by thousands of Anglican and Catholic schools and some Methodist and Jewish schools. Some secularists argue that instead the state should withdraw its funding from all religious schools a kind of "equalising downwards". The issue here is about the legitimacy of religion as a public institutional presence.

Muslims have failed to get the courts to interpret the existing statute on blasphemy to cover offences beyond what Christians hold sacred, but some political support has been built for an offence of incitement to religious hatred, as has existed in Northern Ireland for many years, mirroring the existing one of incitement to racial hatred. (The latter extends protection to cover certain forms of anti-Jewish literature, but not anti-Muslim literature.) Indeed, such a proposal was in the Queen's Speech in October 2004 and reiterated in the new parliament in June 2005. Despite the controversy that this has created, few people seem to have noticed how the law on race is already being stretched to cover religion so that anti-Muslim literature is becoming covered in the way that anti-Jewish literature has been covered from decades.

Positive inclusion of religious groups: The demand here is that the category of "Muslim" should be a category by which the inclusiveness of social institutions may be judged, as they increasingly are in relation to race and gender. For example, employers should have to demonstrate that they do not discriminate against Muslims by explicit monitoring of Muslims' position within the workforce, backed up by appropriate policies and targets. Similarly, public bodies should provide appropriately sensitive policies and staff in relation to the services they provide, especially in relation to (non-Muslim) schools, social and health services; Muslim community centres or Muslim youth workers should be funded in addition to existing Asian and Caribbean community centres and Asian and black youth workers. Again it is a question of the legitimacy of religion as a public institutional presence.

These policy demands no doubt seem odd within the terms of, say, the French or US "wall of separation" between the state and religion, and may make secularists uncomfortable in Britain too. But it is clear that they virtually mirror existing anti-discrimination policy provisions in the UK. Moreover, Muslim assertiveness, though triggered and intensified by what are seen as attacks on Muslims, is primarily derived not from Islam or Islamism but from contemporary Western ideas about equality and multiculturalism. While simultaneously reacting to the latter in its failure to distinguish Muslims from the rest of the "black" population and its uncritical secular bias, Muslims positively use, adapt and extend these contemporary western ideas in order to join other equality-seeking movements. Political Muslims do, therefore, have an ambivalence in relation to multicultural discourses. On the one hand, as a result of previous misrecognition of their identity, and existing biases, there is distrust of "the race relations industry" and of "liberals"; on the other hand, the assertiveness is clearly a product of the positive climate created by liberals and egalitarians. This ambivalence can tend towards antagonism as the assertiveness is increasingly being joined by Islamic discourses and Islamists around the world.

A panicky retreat to a liberal public-private distinction

The emergence of a "politics of difference" out of and alongside a liberal assimilationist equality created a dissonance. Similarly, the emergence of a British Muslim identity out of and alongside ethno-racial identities has created an even greater dissonance because it challenges the hegemonic power of secularism in British political culture, especially on the centre-left. While black and related ethno-racial identities were intrinsic to the

'It is a question of the legitimacy of religion as a public institutional presence'

rainbow coalition of identity politics, this coalition is deeply unhappy with Muslim consciousness.

For some, this rejection is specific to Islam, for many the ostensible reason is that it is a politicised religious identity. Yet this latter objection, if it is taken at its face value, is a reversion to a public-private distinction that many of those on the centre-left have spent two or three decades demolishing. The mix-up can lead secular multiculturalists to find themselves arguing that the sex lives of individuals — traditionally, a core area of liberal privacy — is a legitimate feature of political identities and public discourse. But religion, on the other hand — a key source of communal identity in traditional, non-liberal societies — is to be regarded as a private matter, perhaps as a uniquely private matter. Most specifically, Muslim identity is seen as the illegitimate child of British multiculturalism. Indeed, the Rushdie Affair made evident that the group in British society most politically opposed to (politicised) Muslims weren't Christians, or even right-wing nationalists but the secular, liberal intelligentsia.

What is urgently needed is not a panicky retreat from multiculturalism but to extend its application by providing Muslims with protection from discrimination and incitement to hatred, and the duties on organisations to ensure equality of opportunity, not the watered-down versions of legislation proposed by the European Commission and the UK government. We should target more effectively, in consultation with religious and other representatives, the severe poverty and social exclusion of Muslims. And we should recognise Muslims as a legitimate social partner and include them in the institutional compromises of church and state, religion and politics, that characterise the evolving, moderate secularism of mainstream western Europe, and resist the calls for a more radical, French-style secularism.

A sense of belonging to one's country is necessary to make a success of a multicultural society. But assimilation into an undifferentiated national identity is unrealistic and oppressive as a policy. An inclusive national identity is respectful of and builds upon the identities that people value and does not trample upon them. Simultaneously respecting difference and inculcating Britishness is not a naïve hope but something that is happening and leads everyone to redefine themselves.

International terrorism and neo-conservatism are putting extra strains on democratic, negotiated integration but pessimism about British society's capacity to produce pluralistic (rather than assimilative) integration is premature.

Is faith redefining the race equality project?

Paul Gilroy & Herman Ouseley

Paul Gilroy and Herman Ouseley, two central figures in the development of British race relations, reflect here in an email dialogue on whether the emergence of an increasingly assertive Muslim political identity represents a new departure.

Dear Paul,

There was a time when race relations in Britain could be symbolised by the very simple reference to there being no black in the union jack! White people had the power, control, resources and the empire. Black people were perceived as exotic immigrants doing the shit jobs and disfiguring the landscape, the labour and housing markets.

The empire has long since gone but the other pillars of institutional dominance are well entrenched. No longer can a simple analysis be made of the state of race relations as Britain's changed demography reflects new generations of multi-ethnic origins and heritage.

Over the decades, different groups of people have had to assert themselves to get their grievances heard, sometimes engaging in uprisings.

The most recent bombshells were dropped in the northern towns of Bradford, Burnley and Oldham. The disturbances highlighted the resentment, hatred, ignorance and gulf between poor white and deprived Muslim communities. Just like all previous minority communities before them, sections of the Muslim community have began to assert themselves, and this has forced a redefinition of the race equality project. Faith, belief and religious identity are nowadays regarded as issues warranting explicit consideration in all equality debates. This has weakened some anti-racist strategies. But now, with anti-religious discrimination laws in place, the proposed outlawing of incitement to religious hatred, and a new Equality and Human Rights Commission on the horizon, those communities believe that their concerns are, at least, being acknowledged. This should not, though, disguise the suffering and exclusion which still exist and which require committed leadership and political will to eliminate.

Best wishes, Herman

Dear Herman,

So you think "Muslim assertiveness" is the primary source of our difficult new circumstances? From what you say, outlawing incitement to religious hatred is a convenient governmental device for separating good from bad Muslims. This useful bit of diversity management presumably becomes a price worth paying in order to isolate the hotheads and agitators. Perhaps they'll even be the ones who end up being charged with these exciting new offences.

Bolting official religious sensitivity on to the existing apparatus of "anti-racism" doesn't appear to be a problem for you. For me, it generates exactly the sort of closed and stratified communities it should help to wither away. Processes, identities and feelings that are fluid, complex and internally differentiated become fixed, naturalised and spiritualised.

Britain's official race equality strategies have not failed because they were imprecisely defined, and they will not suddenly start to work better if we can just re-describe more accurately the minorities who are to be their prime beneficiaries.

You're right that in some ways this is a different political game from the one we played during the 1970s, but the logic of expulsion/repatriation remains. The hatreds fester and multiply in the dead zones of the post-industrial economy. The post-colonial condition of the country has intensified its appetite for stable identity just as the historic, cultural content of that identity is being drowned in Americana.

Colluding in the transposition of these large political and economic problems into the language of faith and religion is a defeat and a disaster. It circulates the clash of civilisations argument as facile common sense and empowers only those who imagine they will be able to command these mutually hostile formations.

Our country's political leaders fear being outflanked by the populist right and tabloids, and as a result, have driven the quest for identity to a frenetic new intensity. At the same time, they wrongly imagine that they can manipulate Islamophobia and keep it safely confined within Britain's traditional xenophobia.

They chose not to see that hating Muslims gets articulated together with Europhobia and all the residual, petty, little England-ism which still thinks a combination of whiteness, monarchy and sterling will hold the fort against the rising tide of insecurity, neo-liberal reform and regressive modernisation.

The fantasy of the country as Rourke's Drift must now be dealt with explicitly. We need leaders who will be brave enough to say not that we should stop apologising for the empire, but that it was the empire that made this country what it is, and that we are still dealing with the consequences.

I have been living in the US. If I had a gun, every time I hear the word diversity I would certainly reach for it. The US case shows that managing diversity is just basic code for business as usual. A lucky few will benefit from systematic tokenism and the new varieties of class-based hierarchy that have been brightened up with the gawdy decorations of corporate multiculturalism.

We certainly do need to know what varieties of injury promote the mistaken belief among young British people that an austere, political Islam can be a viable vehicle for their hopes for a better and more just world. More importantly though, we must ask what are the social, economic and cultural conditions that can promote solidarity and mutuality across fluid cultural lines. Better spelling and familiarity with the Book of Common Prayer will not accomplish that.

Perhaps now might be a good time to revive an unfashionable idea of education as a collective benefit, a civilising element which is also a means to build democracy and citizenship?

Paul Gilroy

Dear Paul,

The media-generated fears of "invading" asylum-seekers, Gypsies desecrating the countryside, Muslims asserting their political muscles, and international terrorists about to breach our national defences, make it

'If I had a gun, every time I hear the word diversity I would reach for it'

hard to achieve the much desired inclusive British identity.

Timidity and fear prevent our politicians from taking on the populist right, the tabloids, the Islamophobes and Europhobes. As far as they are concerned, there is a straight choice to be made by everyone. "Diversity, equality and integration" encourages you to conform, compromise and comply in order to gain a level of acceptance. That's supposed to demonstrate successful management of ethnic relations as we see more and more non-white people penetrate the bowels of our institutions.

Two main actions are necessary to counter the bigotry, ignorance and misinformation which characterise race debates in Britain. The first is for political, corporate and community-based leaders to challenge all forms of misinformation and sensationalised media reports that demonise particular groups of people. The second is about what should be happening in our places of learning. Parents are educating and influencing their children with their perceptions, attitudes and limited knowledge, so there is a huge gap to be filled by our nurseries, schools, colleges and universities.

Given that "anti-racist education" is regarded in official quarters as unacceptable indoctrination ("political correctness"), how would you suggest that we might persuade our leaders and educationists to help build democracy and citizenship? Surely that is beyond our reach with the present levels of fear and vulnerability.

Warm regards, Herman

Dear Herman,

I applaud your frankness in saying that your associates in the Blair government are more scared of being called politically correct than they are of the consequences of demonising incomers and spreading fear. If you are right, it is going to be impossible to persuade them of anything that might undermine their grip on power, which comes courtesy of mainstream floating voters in contested constituencies rather than from minority ethnic electorates.

The currency of identity shows this is not a rational debate in which one can score points, so persuasion really isn't the right word. It might help if we appreciate that the problems that derive from unacknowledged colonial crimes and unresolved imperial histories aren't for Britain alone. Similarly divisive issues exist in other post-imperial nations, from France to Japan.

The first things our leaders might gain from this shift are increased moral authority and political credibility, locally and beyond.

Secondly, and here we can turn back towards the issue of Islam in Britain, political leaders might also gain some loyalty and support from disenchanted and excluded people who might otherwise be tempted to dismiss all this talk about diversity and human rights as a bit of opportunistic rhetoric. That elusive, inclusive national solidarity you aspired to can only be built upon trust and an acknowledgment of the damage done by racism in the past.

This may sound like the dreaded "political correctness", but it is only racism which holds all British Muslims responsible for the wrongs perpetrated in the name of that faith by a tiny minority. Diversity is to be found within groups as well as between them.

It's odd that Brits find it comforting to imagine that the US stands for the future of race politics, that they are ahead and that we are behind. The ghastly figures of Colin and Condi are still being wheeled out by people who should know better. I think it would be more productive to reverse that flow.

Forms of intermixture, interdependence and interculture have happened spontaneously in Britain. Though overlooked by governments, these developments might actually contribute to a less embattled future for Europe than the one that the US models supposedly provide.
Paul Gilroy

Dear Paul,

We are now down to the realities of "self interest". Political leaders will examine the mantra of "what's in it for me" before sticking their necks out to tackle racism and xenophobia. But will increased moral authority and political credibility, locally and beyond, be enough?

The disturbances in the northern towns in 2001, involving disadvantaged Muslims and poor white people, revealed the paucity of intermixture, interdependence and intercultural relations between groups inhabiting the same spaces in their local neighbourhoods. Later explorations showed that young white people and young Muslims in those areas were crying out for better teaching, more learning, and the opportunities to mix with people different from themselves.

There is a large comprehensive school in the east end of London, with pupils from every conceivable impoverished background. Their collective experiences include excellent teaching and learning environments which give them self-esteem and confidence and facilitate their respect for others. Good communications between staff, pupils, parents and local communities, information sharing, intercultural mixing and learning, combined with effecting leadership are part of the main ingredients for such success. It works! We need to see it replicated elsewhere and to rid ourselves of the notions that people must compromise, conform and comply in order to gain acceptance.
Yours, Herman

Herman,

You sound as though you're groping your way back towards a class-based politics! Of course, the intercultural contacts I am interested in aren't evenly spread across the whole country. My point was that they need to be recognised and given political significance. Let's agree that we need a map of Britain's new political and cultural geography. Those 2001 riots took place before the new context of the US-led "war on terror". Residential segregation and post-industrial economic resentment were not the only triggers. On one side, there was the old conflict with police. On the other, there seems to have been a new kind of antagonism based on envying the identity, cohesion and solidarity of the post-migrancy generations. Excluded whites may even have experienced an "identity deficit" when they discovered that whiteness has lost its prestige and is now worth next to nothing. We must not let the clash of civilisations emerge unchallenged.
Paul Gilroy

Dear Paul,

We can certainly agree on the need for a map of Britain's new political and cultural geography. I also cannot disagree with your analysis about triggers for conflicts.

If I am groping for anything, it is to hang on to those fundamental

'Many young people will respond to the siren call of political Islam which offers them an ascetic response to the erotic dazzle of consumer culture'

things that work for disadvantaged communities, including demonised communities such as Muslims and asylum seekers, while we await the emergence of the political leadership with the necessary bottle to challenge the status quo.

Hang in there!!!

Warm regards, Herman

Herman,

These are very dangerous times. The British history, which our generation helped to shape, now offers valuable lessons about how to get along convivially in a multicultural polity. If New Labour leaders aren't interested in those fruits of long struggle, we should be able to leapfrog them and share the lessons with governments in other places where young people magically remain "immigrants" three generations after their grandparents migrated!

I know you don't just want to wait for our leaders to find the courage to act. Perhaps we need an infusion of courage, too. In the meantime, Britain's jails are brimful of Reids and Moussaouis. Many young people will respond to the siren call of political Islam which offers them an ascetic and strongly ethical response to the erotic dazzle of consumer culture. Fundamentalism's oversimple solutions will harness the disenchantment that grows with their marginalisation and their hopelessness.

So there must be more to citizenship than bullying asylum seekers to get their spelling right and learn their kings and queens. Active citizenship requires knowledge of the past that is not defensive about imperial crimes, and an openness to the multicultural future. Education is fundamental. I see another key to success in a political outlook that does not counterpose solidarity and diversity so that more of one means less of the other.

Paul Gilroy

We do not always choose our identity —sometimes it is imposed

Gary Younge

Published
21/01/05
The Guardian

Last year, a Muslim reader with a wife and three daughters wrote to me to say that two of his girls voluntarily wear the hijab whereas his wife and one other do not. "This is imposed from outside as much as inside," he wrote. "The girls used to consider themselves Pakistani, until they visited Pakistan... They could not consider themselves British because the external world told them they weren't. So their identity became 'British Muslim'. Not a religious revival, but an establishment of identity. Since 9/11 however, they will not relinquish the 'headgear'. It would be a sign of defeat. Whilst worn, it symbolises resistance."

At any one time we have access to many identities, including race, sexuality, gender, nationality, class and religion. Far from being neutral, these identities are rooted in material conditions that confer power and privilege in relation to one another. These power relations, however, are not fixed. They are fluid in character, dynamic by nature and, therefore, complex in practice.

The decision as to which identities we assert, when we want to assert them and what we want to do with them, is ours. But that decision does not take place in a vacuum. It is shaped by circumstance and sharpened by crisis. We have a choice about which identities to give the floor to, but at specific moments they may also choose us.

Where Muslim identity in the west is concerned, that moment is now. In the abstract, Islam is, of course, just one more religion like any other. Those who follow it are neither better nor worse, neither more peaceful nor more warlike, and no more or less deserving of special consideration than anybody else.

But in the real world, Muslim identity has been singled out for particular interrogation in the west. Muslims have been asked to commit to patriotism, peace at home, war abroad, modernity, secularism, integration, anti-sexism, anti-homophobia, tolerance and monogamy, to name but a few. Most of these things are excellent and should be fought for vigorously on principle. But Muslims are not being asked to sign up to them because they are good or bad in themselves, but as a precondition for belonging in the west at all.

The fact that these values are still being contested in the rest of society is, it seems, irrelevant. No other established community is having its right to live here challenged in a comparable way.

In January 2005, an amateur rugby league match in West Yorkshire ended in chaos after fans shouted racist abuse at a black player, brawled and then allegedly fired an air gun. The player, Lee Innes, was sufficiently integrated and secularised to serve his country in the armed forces and represent it at a national level. That did not stop the referee from advising him to play on the other wing, away from his tormentors on the touchline.

In the end, the game was abandoned. Such episodes prompt not outrage, but a resigned shrug. The fundamentalism was racial, not religious. But

79960

nobody was asking what white people should commit to if they want to remain in a multicultural country.

The truth is that Islam is no longer a religion like another, any more than Catholicism is in Northern Ireland or Judaism was in Nazi Germany. Forces both global and local have shifted its meaning beyond personal faith to a highly politicised identity. It is up to Muslims how much prominence they wish to give to this identity. They do not choose how much prominence others wish to assign to it.

It is not their choice to be disproportionately unemployed, underpaid, under attack and under suspicion in Britain, or to see land and resources once owned by Muslims stolen in the Middle East, their people bombed in Afghanistan and Iraq or their young men and women imprisoned and humiliated in Guantánamo Bay, Belmarsh, Basra and Abu Ghraib. In all of this, the terrorist attacks of September 11 — the choice of a handful of Muslims — should be seen not as a turning point but part of a continuum.

So the answer to the valid question, "Why should we treat Islam any differently?" is at least in part, "Because Islam has been mistreated differently." This does not absolve Muslims or anybody else from the individual responsibility they must take for their choices about the role they wish to play in British society. But let us not pretend that those choices are not constrained or that those questions are asked of everyone.

This interrogation, say some, is the price Muslims must pay for living in a developed western society with secular values. And so the guardians of a mythic British identity have moved from gatekeepers to a nation of shopkeepers. But their demands prompt three questions: Who sets the price? Is it non-negotiable? And if so, what price do we all pay if Muslims, or anybody else, decide to pass on the offer?

'The truth is, Islam is no longer a religion like another, any more than Catholicism is in Northern Ireland'

We've ditched race for religion

Safraz Manzoor

Published
11/01/05
The Guardian

It is something of a cliche to cite the popularity of curry as evidence of the success of multiculturalism. Those hungry for a metaphor for the benefits of immigration delight in explaining that curry is a British dish. The fact is used to illustrate how Asians have happily fashioned a very British way of being Asian.

This argument first gained traction just as Asian films, books and fashion were starting to make an impact on mainstream culture. It did not seem polite to point out that it was not only curry that was a British creation: the very word "Asian" was also cooked up in this country. It went largely unnoticed at the time but, as I discovered while making a radio documentary, there has been a sharp rise in the number of Asians who are rejecting the label in favour of a religious identity. This growth in religious affiliation is greatly significant and offers both challenges and opportunities for wider society.

The term Asian was coined in 1948 by British administrators working in colonial Kenya to describe citizens of newly independent India and Pakistan. It was brought into this country 20 years later with the arrival of Kenyan Asians. Their arrival coincided with a British civil rights movement that was heavily influenced by the US.

Those fighting for racial equality here believed their cause would gain if all people of colour fought under the single political term "black". During the 70s the immigrant communities settled and began facing different cultural questions. Describing them all as black no longer felt useful. Thus the word Asian, which had been a bureaucratic classification, was promoted to a cultural term.

Pakistanis, Indians and Bangladeshis realised that it was an expedient phrase, but Asian continued to gain mainstream currency with the success of films such as East is East and programmes like Goodness Gracious Me.

It became cool to be Asian. Despite its fragile origins Asian, seemed to be solidifying into something that was clear, distinct and tangible.

It took a catastrophe to remind us that the word obscured as much as it illuminated and to expose just how much it hid. The impact of 9/11 on the US and international security is well known. Less noticed has been its impact on Britain's Asian communities. Among the first victims of violence after the attacks on New York and Washington were not Muslims but Sikhs, targeted for their prominent beards and turbans. September 11 changed the type and nature of racial abuse — instead of "Paki", the new term of abuse became "Bin Laden" and "al-Qaida" and the abuse was motivated not by race, but by religion. Hindus and Sikhs, frustrated at being mistaken for Muslims, resolved to assert their own religious identity. In doing so they were sending a message to the rest of the country: we had nothing to do with terrorism and riots — that's the work of those trouble-making Muslims.

For the Muslims, September 11 prompted a resurgence of interest in

Islam with many choosing to embrace their religion as a response to seeing their community vilified and demonised.

The advantage of an identity rooted in race was that it was usefully vague for fighting the big battles against discrimination. Where they had a common interest or enemy, all communities could march under the Asian flag.

But even before the terrorist attacks, the diversity of achievements, assimilation and experience among the Asian communities was threatening to undermine its effectiveness. Hindus and Sikhs were not only outperforming Muslims in education and employment but, because their religion did not forbid alcohol, they were often better integrated.

If Muslims, Hindus and Sikhs are defining themselves by their religion, does it matter to anyone outside these communities? The briefest glance at recent news events would suggest that it does. The complaints from Hindus about the use of a statue of Lord Ganesh as a weapon in Coronation Street and the furore over the performance of Behzti — the play that offended some Sikhs — imply that an exclusively religious identity can be problematic.

And this is the critical question. Is this new religious identity part of an overarching plural identity, or is it exclusive and separate? Put more bluntly, it is a choice between either wanting religion to be a part of an identity or only being defined by religion and arguing that it is more important than any national identity.

How you define yourself tells others a lot about you and who you think you are. Britain's Hindus, Sikhs and Muslims were long defined by others in terms of what they were not: not white, not black, not British. Now, for the first time, identities are being forged from inside the communities and with confidence. These identities emphasise religion but do not necessarily imply disloyalty to being British.

The great danger, however, is that an identity that emboldens the individual can also threaten the wider society. The challenge to ensure that does not happen is one for all Britons — be they Christian, Hindu, Sikh or Muslim.

saf_Manzoor@hotmail.com

'Hindus and Sikhs were not only out-performing Muslims in education and employment but, because their religion did not forbid alcohol, they were often better integrated'

The challenge facing western Muslims

Tariq Ramadan

Published
21/01/05
The Guardian

A feeling of confusion has emerged among "ordinary people", who doubt their ability to preserve their culture and fear being invaded by the customs and values of the other: British citizens with a Muslim background. Doubt and fear commonly provoke reactions of shutting out or of rejection.

British Muslims need to pay more attention to the doubts and fears that their fellow citizens have. They have a duty to establish intellectual, social, cultural and political spaces for the development of trust. This has to begin with engagement in a clear discussion about Islam, about the practices and the values that Muslims promote. Islam is not a culture but a body of principles and universal values. One should not mix up these universal principles with a Pakistani, Turkish or Arabic way of living them.

Islam allows Muslims to adopt aspects of the culture they find themselves in, as long as it does not oppose any clear prohibition specified by their religion. While practising their religion, they can preserve features of their own culture of origin — in the form of richness, not dogma — at the same time as integrating themselves into British culture, which in turn becomes a new dimension of their own identity. No one asks that they remain Pakistani or Arabic Muslims, but simply Muslims; with time, they become Muslims of British culture. This is a process that is not only normal but desirable.

Western Muslims need to find again this intellectual, social and political creativity that has been missing in the Islamic world. British legislation recognises and protects the fundamental rights of all citizens and residents. This common legal framework allows equality within diversity. The presence of Muslims has forced British culture to experience a greater diversity of cultures. A British identity has evolved that is open, plural and constantly in motion, thanks to the cross-fertilisation between reclaimed cultures of origin and the British culture that now includes its new citizens.

Seen from this perspective, the new British Muslim citizenship is enriching for the whole society. Muslims should live it and introduce it to their fellow citizens. Of course, this compels them to come out of intellectual and social ghettos. Living together and building a truly multicultural society does not mean merely being satisfied with the existence of communities of faith or juxtaposed cultures, whose members ignore each other, never meet and remain enclosed within their own universe of symbolic reference points.

Our responsibilities are shared. Members of so-called traditional British society can, at times, doubt their own identity and are frightened. When this happens they need to reject any imprisoning reaction, such as attempting to draw the boundaries of what they may consider to be an authentic British identity. In any period of crisis, the temptation to fall back upon phantoms of national identity is strong as people are carried away by fear, spilling over into the same camp as populists of the extreme right, a phenomenon that we are witnessing all over Europe.

From the Middle Ages, Islam has participated in the building of a European, as well as a British, consciousness in the same way that Judaism or Christianity has. From Shakespeare to Hume, the influences of Islamic civilisation on the literary and philosophical traditions of the time are innumerable. Horizons need to be broadened through the study of these sources, which should be included in the teaching curricula at both secondary and university levels.

This wider, deeper and more subtle understanding of what has moulded British identity throughout history would help all people in this society to open up towards each other and to understand that they are not so very different when judged by their values and hopes. A truly multicultural society cannot exist without an education in the complexity of what shapes us and in the common dimensions that we share with others. The extension of this education consists of developing partnerships in the social and political issues that affect us all, including discrimination (against women, minorities), racism, unemployment. British society must reach this new perception of itself collectively, with its people, all equal before the law, developing multidimensional identities that are always flexible enough to defend their shared values.

It remains imperative to distinguish between social problems and religious challenges. Muslim and non-Muslim citizens alike need to de-Islamise social fractures; unemployment, violence and marginalisation have nothing to do with Islam or Muslim identity.

www.tariqramadan.com

Can Islam make us British?
Dilwar Hussain

Islam lends itself easily to a reading which inspires Muslims living in Britain to set down roots and to live their values in a British context. They can develop loyalties and feel a sense of belonging to Britain just as they did historically in Pakistan, Malaysia or any other traditionally "Muslim" nation, while remaining sincere to Islamic teachings. In the previous chapter Tariq Ramadan wrote, "Islam is not a culture but a body of principles and universal values. One should not mix up these universal principles with a Pakistani, Turkish or Arabic way of living them." In this chapter I hope to briefly indicate how the framework of Islamic thought can create space for a British way of living Islam.

I will explore the Islamic understanding of:

1. The concept of self (who/what am I?)
2. The concept of nation (where am I?)
3. The concept of community (the people I live with).

1. Self

The most influential factor in the Muslim notion of self — and identity — is God and man's relationship with God. For a Muslim, God is One (a concept known as tawhid) and is the Loving and Merciful Creator, Sustainer and the final Judge of all affairs. He is the Lawgiver and the Sovereign (among other attributes), but above all He is Compassionate, Forgiving and Just. And while man is created in a natural state of purity and goodness as vicegerent of God (khalifah), he is capable of weakness and forgetfulness. Man is therefore deputed (istikhlaf), but encouraged to constantly bear his Lord in mind (dhikr) in order to be conscious of God (taqwa) and fulfil his duty as khalifah with justice and diligence. This strong relationship between man and God is designed to keep God at the hub of human life such that the Divine Spirit touches all of man's actions whether this worldly or other worldly (in fact such a division is artificial, for God is the Guide in all affairs). Throughout the ages, God has chosen messengers and given them inspiration and revelation to remind people of these truths. This role now rests with the believers who are encouraged to "call unto good things", to "promote what is right and discourage what is wrong". This spiritual relationship and divine context (rabbaniyyah) sets the scene for man's many and varied roles in life — both public and private.

The Muslim is therefore a subject of God, His deputy, who lives not for himself, but to bring goodness to humanity. A Muslim "self" then, is a deeply spiritual one, but also a socially connected one, with a purpose of stewardship at the macro level, and at the micro level with something to say about notions of the "good" and "bad" in everyday life. This lends itself easily to contemporary discussions of citizenship and engagement of people in civil society as well as political life. The basic objectives (maqasid) of Islamic law (sharia) are designed to protect life, faith, intellect, progeny and property, and are the foundations of an Islamic understanding of social justice. The Qur'an asserts: "...Be just: this is closest to piety..." On a day-to-day basis, Muslims are reminded through the practice of the pillars of Islam: salah (prayer), zakah (alms), sawm (fasting) and hajj (pilgrimage) that actions that are deeply spiritual are not devoid of political consequences. The congregational prayer is often held as an example of a community in harmony with believers standing in rows and functioning as one body. Fasting and charity sensitise the believers to those who lead less fortunate lives and make the war against global poverty a vivid reality. The pilgrimage symbolises equality and the breaking of barriers between nations, classes and tongues.

2. Nation

Traditional Muslim societies were not based on the nation state and it is largely western influence that led to the creation of the many Muslim nations that exist today. In the past, Muslims often lived alongside people of various ethnic and linguistic backgrounds. To this day, the debate goes on as to how legitimate nation states are within Islam. There is a strong transnational connection beyond the nation in the concept of belonging to a single "community of faith", an Ummah. Muhammad said, "the believers are like a single body, if one part aches the whole body responds to the pain." This creates among Muslims an internationalist outlook which has meant that the nation state with its clear boundaries was always difficult to accept. With globalisation, we have seen how the boundaries of the nation state have become more porous, and the internationalism of Islam has been accentuated. We must acknowledge that while Islam frowns upon nationalism as a primary tie of association, there are acceptable forms of adherence to national ties. What Islam is against is the type of nationalism that degenerates into tribalism — of support for one's kinsfolk while putting aside ethical concerns. Or the kind of unthinking nationalism — "My country right or wrong". Islam prohibits such ethical irresponsibility.

During early Islamic history, Muslim scholars derived specific geopolitical terms to define the way in which the law should apply to Muslims living within and outside the Muslim territories. The region that was under Muslim rule was defined as Dar al-Islam (abode of Islam) and the "other" regions were variously described as Dar al-Harb (abode of war), Dar al-Kufr (abode of unbelief), Dar al-'Ahd and Dar al-Sulh (abode of treaty), Dar al-'Amn (abode of security) etc. Many more definitions were coined, but by far the most popular to the scholars were the first two, leading to what Tariq Ramadan calls "a binary vision of the world": the world of Islam and the world of "Others". The implication this had on Islamic jurisprudence was great. Though there were differences among the various schools, most of them disliked that a Muslim should live outside Dar al-Islam. Permission was granted for traders, students, preachers etc, but these were generally seen as exceptions granted for a minimum time. Upon close scrutiny one can deduce that the vital criteria for defining a place as Dar al-Islam were such things as personal security, justice, freedom of worship and avoidance of corruption.

These concepts of non-Muslim Britain as Dar al-Kufr or Dar al-Harb are often cited as obstacles for Muslims living here. But both these concepts were used at a particular time and place and are not part of the primary sources of Islam. They are not relevant in today's globalised world, where Muslims sometimes flee from "Muslim" countries and seek refuge for their very lives and wellbeing in "non-Muslim" countries, or where one finds greater freedom to practise and debate Islam in some "non-Muslim" countries than in some "Muslim" countries.

Another objection cited for Muslims to live in Britain is the conflict between Islamic and British law, but this is true of all parts of the world, as there is no country that applies the sharia in full. However, some scholars argue that the objectives of the sharia are better achieved in a country such as Britain than under despotic rule, as in some parts of the Muslim world.

Finally, another issue raised by some Muslims is that Britain contains many vices and that life here is subject to immoral influences. But the argument about immorality in Britain is exaggerated; as if the Muslim world does not have vice and corruption. Besides, the Prophets were sent to the people throughout the ages who were not "good believers". They were people who were thieves or idol worshippers, or others who oppressed the weak. These were the very people the Prophets called their brethren, their people. If we look closely at the story of Muhammad's life, the Makkah where he lived was dominated by Mushrikin (idol worshippers), yet he felt it was his home. The whole Arab identity was one that revolved around the culture of idolatry, a culture in which baby girls were buried alive and in which drink and promiscuity were common. Yet the Prophet never asked the Muslims to deny their Arab identity, he simply redefined it, redirected it. He took the good things from it, like the honouring of guests, sticking to one's word, chivalry and courage, and discarded what was unacceptable. In fact this is why the Qur'an uses the phrase Amr bil Ma'ruf wa Nahy an il-Munkar, promoting the good and discouraging the wrong. Ma'ruf, commonly translated as "good", actually means in Arabic the things that are common and well known, established in society, the common good. Hence you simply take on those things that are good and leave those that are bad.

3. Community

An Islamic understanding of community is all the people that one lives among, Muslims and non-Muslims alike. The Qur'an relates the story of many messengers, saying that God sent the messengers "to their brethren", who were non-Muslims. The Prophets addressed their community as "my People!" (Qawmi). Hence there is a fraternal relationship between the Muslim and his community, regardless of their belief. The Muslim is one of "them", "they" are part of the Qawm. The Qur'an further clarifies this:

"O mankind! Behold, we have created you from a male and female, and have made you nations and tribes, so that you might come to know one another. Verily the noblest of you in the sight of God is the one who is most conscious of him..."

Thus, plurality of cultures and ethnic groups is acknowledged as a positive factor to enhance human life, rather than be a cause of prejudice. The diasporic existence of Muslims across Europe has meant that community bonds among Muslims have been reified, especially during moments of perceived external pressure, such as the "war on terror". This has served to bring together very different Muslim groups originating from the Indian subcontinent, the Middle East, Africa, Far East Asia and other parts of the world into an imagined community. At times this has turned Muslims away from their non-Muslim co-citizens.

I want to look at one other crucial issue: all these questions of identity and belonging are affected by the emphasis on the Oneness of God which has led Muslims to develop a preoccupation with unity. However, embedded within this unity lies a strong sense of plurality. The acceptance of different faiths, different opinions in fiqh, differences of ethnicity, the encouragement of juristic reasoning, all show this deep sense of pluralism that lies at the heart of Islam. Ultimately, the Qur'an teaches, "...you will be brought back to God and He will show you the truth of the things about which you differed." Meaning that the plurality of opinions held among people in this life will not be resolved and are not meant to be resolved, but we should live with each other in respect. "And if God had willed, He could have made you one people."

There is a dire need in today's Muslim circles and societies to draw upon the pluralistic resources of Islam if the Muslim world is to deal justly with the complexity of diversity within and outside its boundaries. Abdolkarim Soroush, a prominent Iranian thinker on this subject, has advanced the notion of "straight paths" as distinct from the traditional notion of "the straight path" evoked in judgments of orthodoxy and salvation. Yet while such views are the topic of much debate, they remain in a minority at the current time.

Conclusion

Integral to both of these challenges is that Muslim communities become more open to people around them (and vice-versa) so that there is increased mutual understanding and trust, as well as an appreciation of that which is in common — which is far more than that which is different.

The Prophet never isolated himself from the people; he always interacted with them, engaged with them, talked to them, lived with them. It was by seeing his behaviour, his personality that people were most impressed. That's how he began to tackle the Islamophobia that started to arise at his time. When some Muslims talk of "Islamic activism", they often think of proselytising by giving talks, organising conferences, or even going to the neighbourhood, knocking on people's doors or handing out leaflets. Yet faith in Islam requires something far more profound than that; that Muslims live in British society and involve themselves in it fully — that they simply live Islam rather than talk of Islam.

Muslims should have ideas to contribute when it comes to health, education, crime, unemployment, homelessness, and all other areas of life. It would be a shame if they were to sell themselves short by being boxed into a niche, labelled as commentators on "religious matters" or "Islamic matters" alone. The duty of Muslims is not just to ask about their rights and privileges, but to contribute, to help build this society. This is why it is necessary that Muslims understand that this is their society, that the people around them are their people.

If Muslims are to really make their contribution to British society, there must be open and frank dialogue and interaction in both directions. Muhammad was known as "the Trustworthy", "the Honest", "the Truthful". How many Muslims in Britain have the same reputation? Muslims need desperately to sort out their own house and also tackle prejudices that hamper people's views of them. But this too is not enough, for they also have to know their people. How many Muslims have a deep understanding of the history, literature and traditions of Britain? How many actively interact and engage with their non-Muslim co-citizens? Yet how many lead lives that involve almost no interaction with non-Muslims in their day-to-day affairs? Unless Muslims are able to

'Muslims should have ideas to contribute when it comes to health, education, crime, and all other areas of life' feel the pulse of society, they will not talk to people, but talk at them, and their words will have very little effect. This again shows exactly why Muslims need to be in tune with their Britishness. Yes, Islam can make us British... but for this to happen, we have to live Islam not just talk about it.

Part 2
What are we? The new politics of belonging

How are we going to do God?

Sunder Katwala

"Sorry, we don't do God." The secular liberal left's first instinct when facing demands for an increased role for religion in the public sphere has been to refuse to countenance the debate. But simply asserting that Britain is a largely and increasingly secular society, and must therefore remain so, is no longer tenable. If we are to successfully distinguish between the legitimate and illegitimate roles for religion in a democratic society of many faiths and none, then we will need to rethink and redraw the boundaries between religion, the state and public life.

Liberal resistance to reopening this debate has been built on a sense that the question of religion had been long and satisfactorily settled. Increasing secularisation and the declining purchase of the country's Christian heritage was largely accepted, even by mainstream church and religious leaders — particularly those of the Church of England, whose public moderation often bordered on agnosticism. Politically, the Conservative party's traditional role as the "Church of England at prayer" was fading — the extension of Sunday trading in 1986 saw the greatest backbench division of the Thatcher years — the claims of religion were no match for the new liberal capitalism of the right. On the left, the tradition of religious engagement with social justice had long been made on largely secular grounds.

Challenges to this consensus — such as Mary Whitehouse's successful private prosecution for blasphemy against Gay News in 1977 or Ian Paisley's contribution to Ulster's politics — seemed only to confirm a widespread view of its public champions as marginal, and relics from a previous age. This sense of the retreating public role of religion shaped, in part, the context for the Rushdie affair in 1989 — the first time that political claims made on behalf of Islam came to wider public notice. The mainstream response was one of bewilderment and ultimately anger as protests escalated to book burning and threats of violence. There was little engagement or dialogue. The response was largely that "immigrant" communities needed to learn the civilised ways of their "hosts": "that just isn't how we do things here". Religious challenges to free speech — clashes including Sikh protests over the play Behzti and Christian protests against the televising of Jerry Springer: The Opera — have increased liberal fears that a greater role for religion will see a retreat from enlightenment principles and freedoms in the face of absolutist demands that claim to be above public or political scrutiny.

Yet, of course, this claim for a "secular settlement" is a problematic one in a country that retains an established church. As opinion formers declared that our civilised liberal culture treats free speech, rather than religion, as sacred, so making it impossible to ban books which cause offence, it turns out to have a blasphemy law that protects Christianity on the statute book. Britain had come to think of itself as increasingly de facto secular when it was not. It is a strange secular polity where the prime minister appoints the bishops of the Church of England, and where they sit by right in the House of Lords to vote on and amend the laws of the land. The liberal response — "nobody takes any of that seriously anymore" — was not dishonest, given the limited role of the established church in public debates. But it was naturally seen as self-serving and suspicious when used to prohibit new political claims made on religious grounds. In the Rushdie affair, protesters could argue with some justification that it was the particular claim of Islam that was being discriminated against.

What is secularism?

The liberal left is confused by the renewed prominence and new political claims made for religion. While the liberal left prides itself on its enlightenment rationalism, there is no rational defence of a "settlement" that contains such a large element of organised hypocrisy. Part of the confusion is because the challenge is being made by applying to faith the identity politics arguments developed on race and gender, as Tariq Modood has pointed out, which the left has supported over the last 30 years. This disconcerts the liberal left, in part because liberals have not distinguished sufficiently between different forms of, and arguments for, secularism — and risk defending the wrong thing.

The primary objective of those who put forward the secularist perspective is to uphold values of equality, democratic citizenship and human rights — a goal that will be recognised as valid by many people of faith as well as agnostics and atheists. But quite different weak and strong secularist positions are often confused. The first seeks the separation of the state and religion — that the state does not enforce or institutionalise any particular religion, nor discriminate on the basis of religious considerations in its treatment of its citizens. The second, and stronger, secularist claim seeks to separate religion from politics by claiming that religion must be an exclusively private matter, and that religious identities, principles and concerns need to be left outside the door when citizens enter the public space.

The British status quo offers a clear, if half-hearted, breach of the first — valid — principle. The attempt to make the second — considerably more questionable — approach sticks in the face of growing dissent. This is in direct contrast to the United States, a polity which insists on the strict constitutional separation of church and state and yet where religious language suffuses the public sphere. The first approach makes much sense, particularly in multifaith and multi-ethnic societies where the equal treatment of citizens might well be seen to demand the equal treatment of their different religions. But the second demand that citizens must use only secular reasons in public discussion cannot be defended. It demands that religious citizens must abstract themselves from their deepest beliefs in accepting an iron distinction between private beliefs and public values. This is not a condition of equal citizenship but a violation of it. It seeks to set the "rules of the game" for public discourse in a way that decides the central issue of contention between religious and secular worldviews. The justifiable demand that can be made of religious claims and arguments made from a religious perspective is that they are open to challenge by others within the public space, along with the claims of those who wish to argue that religion is dangerous and illegitimate.

> 'Liberals have not distinguished sufficiently between different forms of, and arguments for, secularism — and risk defending the wrong thing'

Towards a new settlement

We therefore need a new settlement. The foundations around which this can be negotiated should be the human rights of all citizens, and the equal treatment of all major religions by public authorities. While these may seem uncontroversial, each of these foundation principles represents a political choice, and either can be challenged. A defence for retaining an established church (while various other religions are either favoured or discriminated against in a range of ways), beyond inertia, could depend on an argument either from history — namely, that Britain has an essentially Christian heritage — or a majoritarian democratic argument based on weight of numbers — that 78% of Britons regard themselves as Christian in the 2001 census. But neither argument offers convincing grounds for giving preferential treatment to one faith over another.

Accepting the principle of equal treatment of religions leaves open many central questions about what this would mean in practice. How far should we seek a US-style strict separation between the state and all expressions of religion? Or would an alternative to this be to offer a greater recognition of all major religions in public life, including some form of "co-establishment" of major religions, in the spirit of Prince Charles's thinking about the future role of the head of state including that of being a "defender of faiths".

Seeking to extend some of the current privileges of the Church of England to different religions would face practical difficulties on a number of particular issues, and would need careful checks to prevent important breaches of human rights principles. But it is perfectly possible to imagine a patchwork and partial "co-establishment" approach.

This might particularly be pursued in terms of the symbolism of the state and public life — what Bagehot called the "dignified" parts of the British constitution. It would be difficult, for example, to see why there should be any objection in principle to a coronation ceremony which sought to symbolise Britain as a multifaith society in all of its colour and flummery, or why public institutions such as parliament, the courts and the army should not offer a range of oaths (including secular versions). The prohibition on the heir to the throne marrying a Catholic would go — and perhaps the requirement for the monarch to be a Protestant, too.

This may well in many ways be a particularly British approach, reminiscent of George Orwell's claims in The Lion and the Unicorn that his new post-revolutionary England "will not be doctrinaire, nor even logical. It will abolish the House of Lords, but quite probably will not abolish the monarchy. It will leave anachronisms and loose ends everywhere, the judge in his ridiculous horsehair wig and the lion and the unicorn on the soldier's cap buttons." A pragmatic empiricism to the relationship between religion and the state will not deliver an entirely coherent blueprint or as clear a distinction as that favoured in principle in the United States — but the outcome will be challenged if it does not seem to be animated by a concern for fairness and equity between faiths and citizens. (At the boundary, the definition of major faiths would be somewhat arbitrary, but this would not present any great difficulty: Jedi Knights and Scientologists need not apply.)

More substantively, if we were to retain a fully or partly appointed upper house, there would be a choice between removing the Church of England's bishops from the House of Lords or alternatively adding senior representatives of other faiths to sit and legislate. It would be preferable

'Extending some of the privileges of the Church of England to different religions would face difficulties on a number of issues' for no religious leaders to sit by right, but for an appointments commission to ensure that different faith and community perspectives are represented, not necessarily through the appointment of religious leaders, but rather by taking religion into consideration as one factor when appointing peers who are experts on a range of areas.

Those who fear the consequences of religious segregation in education for integration, citizenship and a shared society can make the case for abolishing the Church of England, Roman Catholic and Jewish state schools which have long been part of the educational system. But since their abolition is not a practical political proposition, the case for Muslim state schools to be funded by the state is in practice undeniable. The issues of integration and citizenship for faith schools — of all faiths — will then need to be addressed through regulation of the content of the curriculum, admissions policies as well as links between different schools and other, softer initiatives.

By contrast, seeking to extend the blasphemy laws to cover the central tenets of all faiths would be both undesirable as well as practically impossible. It would place unacceptable restrictions on freedom of speech and expression, including, no doubt, religious as well as secular speech since it is likely that different religions would routinely blaspheme against each other.

Hard cases and the limits of human rights

The broad framework outlined here — of equality of religions within a human rights framework — will not resolve the outcome and provide the "right answer" to any particular policy question or clash. These will be the subject of political negotiation and compromise — it might well be that new deliberative spaces, beyond parliament and the courts, should be created to host and interrogate these debates.

Using a human rights framework for the scope and limits for the public recognition of religion will, for some, continue to privilege the individualistic, liberal and secular worldview over religious perspectives. But an emerging culture of human rights — though relatively underdeveloped in Britain — offers a strong and essential basis for the level of consensus necessary to live together in a complex society. In contrast with the claim rejected earlier, namely that religion must be left out of public discourse entirely, claims of human rights and dignity are recognised by all major religions, though this leaves many questions about their content and practical implications. The argument over how claims for human rights are grounded and defended is beyond the scope of this piece. But a rights culture offers only a framework for deliberation — no single right is a trump card that can end discussion — through which conflict can be resolved or contained.

As Michael Ignatieff has written: "The fundamental commitment entailed by rights is not to respect, but to deliberation. The minimum condition for deliberation with another human being is not necessarily respect, merely negative toleration, a willingness to remain in the same room, listening to claims one doesn't like to hear, for the purposes of finding compromises that will keep conflicting claims from ending in irreparable harm to either side. That is what a shared commitment to human rights entails."

The hardest practical cases where religious and non-religious worldviews will continue to clash will include those where free speech causes deep offence, tensions between group and individual rights, and the

'Extending
blasphemy
laws to
cover the
central
tenets of all
faiths would
be both
undesirable
as well as
practically
impossible'

choices that parents can make on behalf of their children. One area of contention will be the scope and limits of the group rights that can be claimed by religious or other communities. Just as western societies have increasingly come to recognise gender, ethnicity and sexuality as central components of cultural identity, this will also be true of faith identities and communities. However, there will be limits to what can be claimed on these grounds because those group rights and identities which are recognised publicly gain that recognition because they are good for the individuals involved. Those individuals must, however, have the freedom of exit: without that, there is no basis on which group rights can and should be granted by a democratic society, an issue that Malicha Malik takes up in her contribution to this book.

Finally, on issues of free speech, the threshold for restricting speech would need to be set very high; it could not be on the grounds of offence, however deeply felt. As Bhikhu Parekh has argued, protesters against Rushdie's book did have regard to the social and political contexts of different countries. While The Satanic Verses was banned in India, no Muslim call to ban the book was made in the United States where it would clearly have failed on first amendment rights. So the anachronistic British law against blasphemy did offer grounds for British Muslims to believe that it was reasonable to ask for a ban. Redrawing the boundaries between religion and the state will not settle such hard disputes but the neglect of religious questions — almost the only part of Britain's constitution not to be reformed by the post-1997 Labour government — now needs to be reversed if we are to create a legitimate and equitable framework to contain and resolve these tensions and differences.

New allies: the left must make peace with an old enemy

Seumas Milne

Published
16/12/04
The Guardian

For more than two centuries, since its emergence from the French revolution, the political left has been in conflict with religion. From the epic 19th-century struggle of republicans against clericalism to the militant atheism of 20th-century communism, leftwing movements regarded organised religion as a pivotal prop of the established order, an ally of the powers that be, from tsarist Russia to Tibet.

And as children of the enlightenment, the bulk of the left saw religious belief itself as little more than a superstitious hangover from the pre-scientific age, preaching social deference — the rich man in his castle, the poor man at his gate — while diverting the oppressed from collective action in the here and now to the hope of justice in the afterlife. This was the background against which Spanish priests were targeted as cheer-leaders of Francoite fascism in the 30s, while Soviet churches were turned into museums of atheism and Enver Hoxha decreed the outright abolition of religion in Maoist Albania in the 60s.

But many of the conditions that gave rise to earlier leftwing hostility to religion have eroded, as religion itself has declined in Europe and else-where. The bonds between religious institutions and ruling elites have been weakened, while the radical strands within religion — which were always present, not least in the core religious texts themselves — have grown stronger, typified by the egalitarian Christian liberation theology movement. Even the most established religious authorities have become sharply critical of the global system, challenging inequality and western military aggression. During the 1990s the Pope, who played a central role in the rollback of communism, was one of the few international figures who could be heard speaking out against the new capitalist order. Religion cannot but find itself in conflict with the demands of an ever more voracious capitalism to dominate social and personal life, which religion has traditionally seen as its own sphere of influence.

Of course, shifts within religion have not only been in one direction: from Vatican opposition to contraception in Aids-blighted Africa, the rise of Hindu nationalism or the advance of rightwing US evangelicals, there have also been negative trends. But the loosening of the links between religion and state and economic power has allowed the secular left to work with the religious in a way that was far more difficult in the past.

It is the insurgent spirit of political Islam, however, that has brought the issue of how progressive movements should relate to religion to a head. Modern Islamism has flourished on the back of the failures of the left and secular nationalists in the Muslim world, and has increasingly drawn its support from the poor and marginalised. That has had an impact on the outlook of Islamist groups that not long ago were backed by the west as conservative ballast for its client states in the Middle East. Meanwhile, Muslims find themselves at the sharpest end of conflict with the new imperial world order, from Iraq and Afghanistan to Chechnya, central Asia and Saudi Arabia — subject to invasion, occupation and

> 'Religion cannot but find itself in conflict with the demands of an ever more voracious capitalism to dominate social and personal life'

western-backed tyranny unparalleled in any other part of the globe. Across western Europe, Muslims are the target of an unprecedented level of hostility and attacks, while segregated at the bottom of the social hierarchy — now forming, for example, the majority of the prison population in France.

But for showing solidarity and working with Muslim organisations — whether in the anti-war movement or in campaigns against Islamophobia — leftwing groups and politicians such as the London mayor, Ken Livingstone, are now routinely damned by liberal secularists (many of whom have been keen supporters of the war in Iraq) for "betraying the enlightenment" and making common cause with "Islamofascists", homophobes and misogynists. The pitch of these denunciations has been heightened further by the government's plan to introduce a new criminal offence of incitement to religious hatred. This measure would extend to the most vulnerable community in the country the very modest protection already offered by race-hate legislation to black people, Jews, Sikhs and all religious communities in Northern Ireland. It is not a new blasphemy law — it would not lead to a ban on Monty Python's Life of Brian film nor rule out jokes about Ayatollah Khomeini's contact lenses, or cover ridicule or attacks on any religion (unlike the broader Australian legislation) — but would only outlaw incitement of hatred against people because of their faith.

Many arguments now deployed against this proposal by an unholy alliance of evangelical Christians, xenophobes, the British National Party, secular literalists and libertarians were also used against anti-racist legislation in the 60s and 70s. And none of the public opposition seems to have included the consequent logical demand that protection for Jews, Sikhs and religious people in Northern Ireland be repealed, which only underlines the noxious nature of debate about Islam in Britain.

At its most rational, opposition to protection for Muslims and other religious groups is based on the argument that whereas race is about biology, religion is a set of ideas which can be adopted or discarded at will. But in reality, just as ethnicity isn't mainly an issue of genetics, religion isn't only a question of beliefs: both are also about culture and identity. In Britain, religion has increasingly become a proxy for race. It hasn't escaped the attention of racists that many people in Britain who a generation ago would have regarded themselves as Pakistani or Bangladeshi now see themselves primarily as Muslims — nor that targeting Muslims is a way round existing race hate legislation, as well as drawing on the most poisonous prejudices and conflict of our era.

By the same token, for the secular left — which is about social justice and solidarity if it is about anything — not to have stood with British Muslims over Islamophobia or the invasions of Afghanistan and Iraq would have been the real betrayal. It is not, and has not been, in any way necessary to compromise with social conservatism over women's or gay rights, say, to have such an engagement; on the contrary, dialogue can change both sides in positive ways. But it is a chronic flaw of liberalism to fail to recognise power inequalities in social relations — and the attitude of some liberals to contemporary Islam reflects that blindness in spades.

Outright opposition to religion was important in its time. But to fetishise traditional secularism in our time is to fail to understand its changing social meaning. Like nationalism, religion can face either way, playing a progressive or reactionary role. The crucial struggle is now within religion rather than against it.

Leave God out of it
Polly Toynbee

The trouble with all religions is that they refuse to understand or accept the validity of atheism. So when atheists call for keeping all religion right out of the affairs of state, each sect and cult takes it as a personal affront to their particular faith.

Far worse, if, in the British context, believers perceive their faith to be part of their racial identity, this can cause a toxic misunderstanding. That is how the mistaken concept of "Islamophobia" became a synonym for racism. When someone calls an atheist an Islamophobe they tar them with the brush of racism in an attempt to silence their anti-religious views.

When atheists protest against the rise of religious influence on the state, all the religions hasten to gather together to protect their collective interest. Whether this is over the bizarre ring-fencing of air time for all religions on the BBC, the growing number of religious state schools or proposals to add yet more religious leaders to the House of Lords, they rally round in a huddle and support one another. To the outsider this is not only puzzling but suspect, since each of them lays claim to a unique mystical truth, the one and only path to salvation. Only extreme fundamentalists want to destroy the infidels' other faiths, but the moderates still regard the others as essentially misguided, even if spiritually on the same wavelength. The atheist is left to ponder why they all conspire to promote the idea that any religion is always better than none, however alien that religion and its culture may be to their own. So archbishops, cardinals, imams, rabbis and the rest tend to conspire in an unlikely coalition to promote any belief against the common enemy — unbelief.

Recently, though, a Muslim colleague on a committee we both serve on came up to me at the end of a meeting to praise me for a strong attack I had written on Pope John Paul II: "It was good to see a religion other than Islam criticised for once," he said. I protested that I have often and always been a severe critic of Christianity, but he was convinced Christians were always immune, due to the archaic blasphemy laws. Atheistic views had been invisible to him: the religious have a habit of noticing only slights to their own faith.

That was, I suppose, how I came to be named as "most Islamophobic media personality" in malicious awards handed out by the Islamic Human Rights Commission in 2004. This is the poisonous company they put me in: other awards went to Nick Griffin, leader of the BNP, George Bush, Ariel Sharon and Jacques Chirac. The result was a savage bombardment of emails from all over the world, many of them threatening, all of them extremely abusive. Just as unpleasant was the stream of emails mainly from fundamentalist Hindus filled with desire to kill all Muslims, as if I was on their side.

What brought all this down on my head? I had challenged the notion of "Islamophobia", warning of the danger to free speech of trying to stifle criticism of a religion by denouncing it as akin to racism. As a long-time

'The religious have a habit of noticing only slights to their own faith'

associate of the National Secular Society, I have always opposed any infiltration of religion into the state. Wherever religion gets its hands on temporal power, freedom is at risk. It has taken centuries and an enlightenment to forge a division between the two, because theocracy is always lethal.

Yet there are many Muslims who interpret Islam as a belief system that holistically conjoins the two. Democracy, some Muslims say, is itself un-Islamic and sharia law imposed by imams is the only law. Now it must be permissible to challenge such a view without being accused of ethnocentric racism. Certain rights and liberties are universal — or at least I have the right to argue so and no one should take mortal offence or claim it is some kind of racism to say so. That is freedom of speech.

Demanding a total separation of religion and state inevitability leads to conflict with the Church of England, Britain's established religion, with 25 bishops as part of the legislature, making law in the House of Lords. The bishops are profoundly opposed to giving up that status in all the debate about reform of the Upper House. Instead, they want to entrench their position by proposing permanent seats for leaders of the other major faiths as well. The idea that perhaps double the number of religious leaders will fill the Lords is outrageous in this, the most secular of all nations. But to deny the other religions equality looks unjust and to many it looks like racial exclusion.

The same dilemma arises over schools. Britain is the least religious country in the world — and yet a third of its state schools are run by religions, mainly Christian. This is partly historical accident as the churches owned schools before the state took over education. But in a travesty of the national character, this Labour government has created another 60 religious schools. A few of them are Muslim, a few Jewish. While the Christians have their sectarian schools, who could deny this right to all the faiths? That really would smack of racism.

Yet the truth is that for quite different reasons, both Christian and Muslim schools are profoundly socially divisive. While Christian schools contain some believers, most parents are not, though some pretend. Research has shown how most (but not all) religious schools have better results because through overt or unconscious methods they socially select enough of their pupils to ensure they screen out the worst children. Church schools tend to be the middle-class schools in an area. Sociologically this class identity is far more important than the religious identity, and it is seriously socially divisive.

Muslim and Jewish schools are a social danger too, because they also keep communities apart: children educated together learn to live with each other. It is already shocking that in some northern towns, by geographic racial segregation, it happens that there are all white and all Muslim schools in separate areas. But to deliberately encourage separate education by allowing more state Muslim, Jewish, Catholic or any other religious schools only stores up real trouble for the future. Look no further than the catastrophe of religiously segregated schools in Northern Ireland. Why make that mistake all over again with the Muslim community now?

But of course nothing will be done because politicians will not dare dismantle the church schools for fear of the wrath of the white middle classes who have done so well out of them. And while the Christians (or those pretending to be) choose segregation, how can anyone deny the Muslims?

'Wherever religion gets its hands on temporal power, freedom is at risk'

It is becoming increasingly difficult to raise these questions in a climate where the Muslim community feels under threat from everyday racism, virulently stirred up again by the aggressive anti-asylum and immigration campaign fought by the Conservatives and BNP. Meanwhile Muslims also feel threatened by anti-terror laws that risk exposing them to official harassment on the grounds of their religion. To these threats, the liberal instinct is to close ranks and offer maximum support.

But there are profound dilemmas for liberals here. Those Muslim communities where women are subjugated entirely to male control cannot be left to their own devices. Women who cannot leave the home, cannot take jobs, never get the chance to learn English or live free lives deserve liberation, as British citizens. Cultural sensitivity does not extend to tactfully drawing a veil over British citizens kept in near-captivity in some communities. But liberals and progressives are embarrassed and, in a kind of softening of the brain, are afraid to find themselves linked with BNP prejudice. They prefer to say nothing. Teachers and social workers are too often silenced when they see girls' lives and futures severely restrained.

The left of the George Galloway tendency turns a convenient blind eye on the question of women. Women's freedoms did not feature much in his campaign. The far left has preferred to espouse the extreme Islamist cause, which is surely bizarre. It is the passionate anti-Americanism of some Islamic strands that makes them an exciting potential ally for the revolutionary left: "My enemy's enemy" is always welcome and extremists in the Muslim world are the best global anti-Americans at the moment. The hard left always has a natural bloodlust for terrorism wherever it is, whatever the cause. Cordite and the blood of martyrs excites them, without sharing an iota of the Muslim faith or way of life.

Of course most British Muslims are not terrorist sympathisers at all. That being so, it is unclear why the moderate Muslim Council of Britain has not at tense moments spoken out more often and more fiercely against terror: no doubt it is that collective sense of a community living together in some fear not wishing to divide itself, as often with the Catholics in Northern Ireland. But it has been a tragic mistake for Muslim community leaders not to have been as vociferously indignant about the threat of terror from some groups within as they have been about the draconian anti-terror laws.

The squirming of the liberal conscience over Islam has been not altogether edifying. It should not be too difficult for progressives to see the difference between individual freedoms and the collective good. The hijab question was never a problem for British liberals in a country with an established church: French secular history makes it a different matter for them. Of course girls should be allowed to wear the religious/cultural symbols they choose, and sensible schools have created uniforms together with the majority of their Muslim parents and children.

Tolerance is the aim. But that does not include tolerating intolerance. Members of Muslim families are each independent British citizens and must have the same freedoms. Tolerance also means that all religions must be open to critique. If some Muslims choose to interpret the Qu'ran as an incitement to violence and hatred, the way Ian Paisley uses the Bible to incite sectarian hatred against Catholics, then it is not "Islamophobic" to protest. It is essential that we have the freedom to speak out against religious fanatics, cultists and separatists whoever they are.

Is Britain really Islamophobic? The great test is coming soon over the admission of Turkey to the European Union. The French and Germans voters are already showing signs of strong resistance. But the British government is rightly a loud advocate for welcoming Turkey in. Here is a model nation that is Islamic in culture but secular in government, showing the way the secular and religious can coexist. Kemal Attaturk, the revolutionary moderniser, long ago pointed the way forward for Islamic nations.

For economic and social reasons it will take a while before Turkey is sufficiently aligned, but it is taking giant steps in reforms to make itself eligible for admission. If Europe shuts its doors, that will proclaim we are cultural isolationists and xenophobes, a Christendom still locked in ancient crusader combat with the Islamic world.

That is what Muslim communities living within Europe feel now: it is vitally important that we demonstrate to them that they and their religions are as much a part of the modern European identity as any other in the great migrant melange of European blood and culture. Perhaps if we succeed in this essential symbolic gesture, the Muslim communities all over Europe will settle into a more comfortable and less fearful state of mind. Perhaps the absurd charge of "Islamophobia" will no longer be used as a weapon against atheists and secularists.

In the mean time it is important for anti-racists to stand like Voltaire, ready to defend Muslims, their right to be here and their right to practise their beliefs against the tidal wave of "swamped-by-aliens" resentment unleashed by the Conservatives and the BNP. But Muslims themselves need to distinguish between those of us who exercise the right to criticise all religions, theirs included, without smearing all critics as racists.

Stop this folly now. There is no need to sacrifice free speech in order to protect British Muslims

Timothy Garton Ash

Published
19/02/05
The Guardian

Like a man trying to stop a leaking wastepipe with a priceless Raphael drawing, the government is about to do great damage in the cause of averting damage. This impending folly is its proposed legislation on "incitement to religious hatred". Everyone who cares about free speech — the oxygen of so many other freedoms — must shout now to stay the government's hand and prevent it pushing through parliament this ill-conceived, badly worded, dangerous piece of law.

But first of all, let's acknowledge that there is a problem with that leaking wastepipe. Particularly since the 9/11 terrorist attacks, the effluent of human hatred in western societies, including Britain, has flowed more strongly against people rightly or wrongly described as "Muslims". This ranges from casual remarks to serious agitation by the xenophobic right.

The law has already been strengthened to address this problem. When Mark Norwood, an activist of the British National Party, displayed in the window of his flat in Gobowen, a small town in Shropshire, a poster with the words "Islam out of Britain" next to a photograph of the World Trade Centre in flames, he was tried and convicted under a 2001 amendment to the 1998 Crime and Disorder Act. This extended the offence of causing alarm or distress to include cases that are "racially or religiously aggravated". The conviction was recently upheld by the European court of human rights.

However, as Fiona McTaggart (then the responsible Home Office minister) stressed in an interview for this column, while the law prevents people like Norwood from publicly offending or harassing Muslims, it does not yet stop them from inciting their followers to do so. In a curious anachronism, the British legislation on incitement to racial hatred protects Jews and Sikhs, but not Muslims. That inconsistency is a source of understandable grievance to British Muslims.

Unfortunately, the government's proposed solution to this real problem will only make things worse. Its new schedule 10 to the serious organised crime and police bill, which went through its third reading in the House of Commons in February this year, despite strong objections, and now goes to the House of Lords, would criminalise a speech, publication or performance which is "likely to be heard or seen by any person in whom they are... likely to stir up racial or religious hatred". Religious hatred is defined as "hatred against a group of persons defined by reference to religious belief or lack of religious belief". That would seem to cover all the bases, especially since "religious belief" is nowhere otherwise defined.

This loose talk cast as law is dangerous in several ways. While the government insists it's intended only to prevent incitement against persons, not against religions, the line between criticising believers and criticising beliefs is unclear. Race and religion are quite different. There is no possible rational objection to blackness. There are many possible rational objections to religion, whether Christianity, Judaism, Hinduism or

Islam, and some of the greatest thinkers in modern history have held them.

Moreover, the legislation does not require proof of the intent to "stir up" religious hatred, merely the effect. One could credibly argue that the effect (though obviously not the intention) of the publication of Salman Rushdie's The Satanic Verses was to stir up religious hatred, first among and then against British Muslims. "Oh no," cry government spokespersons, "of course this law would never be used against something like The Satanic Verses." But challenged on this point in the Commons debate, Khalid Mahmood, a Labour MP from Birmingham, said: "In the context of Salman Rushdie, the issue was the abusive words that he deliberately used, which were written in phonetic Urdu..." Such issues, he suggested, should be tested in the courts.

> 'The task of the government in all liberal democracies is to strike a balance between two great public goods, freedom and security'

The effect of this law, if passed, could be to deter writers, actors or film-makers from risking offensive portrayals of Islam and other religions. Indeed, as Kenan Malik points out in the latest issue of Prospect magazine, it might even encourage offended groups to mount riotous protests. For they might think that such public disorder would be evidence in court that religious hatred had, in effect, been stirred up. While ministers hasten to assure us that prosecutions under this legislation are likely to be few and far between, a single case could produce a martyr for the far right. If, however, there are no prosecutions, the government will have raised expectations among Mr Mahmood's constituents that will then be disappointed.

Why do it, and why now? A cynical interpretation is that, in the run-up to a general election, New Labour is trying to woo back Muslim voters alienated by Blair's stance on the Iraq war, the detentions without trial of British Muslims in Belmarsh prison and Guantánamo, and so on. Fiona McTaggart argued to me, with passion, that it is about the historically vital task of making the Muslim community feel secure, included and at home in Britain. One can see how, for a committed Labour minister, the two things could merge in the mind.

Yet to impute motives for which one has no hard evidence is unfair, so let's take the government's case on its own terms. It's still wrong. In a letter addressed to Salman Rushdie, as a leading voice in a formidable group of objectors put together by English PEN (the association of writers), McTaggart wrote: "Writers and artists, like yourself, are rightly concerned about freedom of expression. The government's prime concern is the safety and security of communities." No! That may be her prime concern, as the minister for race equality, community policy and civil renewal, but the task of the government, in all liberal democracies, is to strike a balance between two great public goods, freedom and security. Here they are proposing too great a risk to freedom, for too uncertain a gain in security.

There's a simple solution to hand. In the Commons last week, the Liberal Democrat MP Evan Harris proposed an amendment, originally drafted by the distinguished human rights lawyer Anthony Lester, which would change the law on incitement to racial hatred to include "reference to a religion or religious belief or to a person's membership or presumed membership of a religious group as a pretext for stirring up racial hatred against a racial group". Basta. Problem addressed.

If New Labour wants to go further, then, in its historic third term, it can take two larger steps towards building a society that is both free and multicultural. It can abolish our ludicrously outmoded blasphemy law, which (notionally) protects only the Church of England. And it can disestablish the Church of England, thus allowing Prince Charles, an energetic patron of the Oxford Centre for Islamic Studies, to be what he has said he wants to be: defender of faith, not the Faith.

Meanwhile, there's this bad law to be seen off. When the Lords have sent it back to the Commons, parliament has adjourned for the election, and Labour has won again, with the help of those Muslim votes, the government should quietly drop it — and pass instead the practical, careful, precise Lester/Harris amendment. That's an appropriate piece of stout paper to stop the leak in the wastepipe. And we will save our Raphael of free speech.

The bill on the incitement to religious hatred was withdrawn when parliament was dissolved and the election of May 2005 was called. It was reintroduced by the government in June 2005.

In the grip of panic: global conflict has inflamed the problems of British Muslims

Jonathan Freedland

Published
22/01/05
The Guardian

These questions have long smouldered — but now they're on fire. For several years a bunch of knotty problems have confronted British Muslims. They were debated at a Guardian conference earlier in the week. But what's given them a new, radioactive charge are events thousands of miles away from Oldham, Bradford and Burnley, events over which British policymakers are almost powerless. The debate about British Islam is not confined to these islands and will not be settled here alone. It is suddenly part of a much larger, international story.

Take the word "Asian". One fascinating phenomenon laid bare in this week's conversations was the decline of that term. Those who used to wear the Asian label are now ditching it, as Safraz Manzoor made clear in his piece. He cited the young woman who told him that, these days, she preferred to announce herself as a Hindu. Why? Because if she was just an "Asian" she might be confused for a Muslim — and therefore regarded as a terrorist.

This is the rocket fuel that has been tipped over the already tinder-dry terrain of Islam's place in Britain. There was discrimination, tension, poverty and segregation before. But what's shifted this cluster of problems from the realm it used to inhabit — the concern of social workers and urban policy types — into one of the most vexed questions confronting contemporary British life is the perception of Islam as a global phenomenon. And not just a phenomenon: a threat.

Put simply, young Pakistani lads may have been hassled on the streets before, but now they are seen as "Muslims", agents of a terrifying global menace. Now it's not just about white resentment of Bangladeshis' housing allocation from the local council — it's about white fears of worldwide, Islamist terrorism. Before 9/11 the familiar racist charge was that outsiders threatened to change the traditional "British" way of life. Now that fear has been joined by a new suspicion: that these outsiders might want to kill anyone they can.

And the fear extends far beyond sink estates and blighted towns. It courses through society from the bottom to the top. Flick through the comment pages of the right-leaning newspapers and it won't be long before you find an essay written not by an unemployed white lad in Leeds but by a learned, well-paid commentator in the south-east, outlining the danger the fundamentally alien culture of Islam poses to the "rest of us".

Several of those present at this week's dialogue argued that the state subtly reinforces that message. For all Tony Blair's praise of the Qur'an and of Islam as a religion of peace, these speakers said the practical effect of Belmarsh and Guantànamo Bay, even citizenship tests and ID cards, was to cast one group of Britons as the enemy within — on the wrong side of the war against terror.

An article by Kenan Malik in the latest edition of Prospect magazine challenges all that head on, insisting that Islamophobia is a "myth" and

> **'Young Pakistani lads may have been hassled on the streets before, but now they are seen as agents of a terrifying global menace'**

that the number of recorded attacks against British Muslims is in fact far lower than popularly imagined. Malik dismisses the widespread assumption that Muslims make up the majority of those stopped and searched under anti-terrorist laws: he says Asians make up 14% of those arrested — still disproportionately large, but not the 90-plus percentages some Muslim leaders have claimed.

Even if he is right at street level, he surely cannot deny the change in the climate of opinion. The rightwing press is in the grip of a moral panic, constantly serving up new theories to shore up the now familiar thesis that the west and Islam are locked in a clash of civilisations. Admittedly, events in the world don't help. Palestinian suicide bombing, the school siege at Beslan and beheadings in Iraq all fuel the image of an Islamism that shows no mercy.

British Muslims have got caught up in this and it is affecting their lives, here in this country. For they stand accused — explicitly by the BNP, tacitly by more respectable others — of being a fifth column, a homegrown wing of a global movement bent on terrorising the west.

What this amounts to is an external pressure, a big finger pointing at British citizens and calling them "Muslim". But there is also an internal pull, drawing men and women to embrace a label they might once have eschewed.

Testimony from this week's conference spoke of young people from Pakistani and Bangladeshi families who feel no connection with an "old country" they may never have seen, and who therefore reject the label associated with it: they are not from Pakistan, so why should they be called Pakistanis? But nor can they easily swap "Pakistani" for "British" when so many of them feel rejected, or at least suspected, by Britain. "Muslim" has stepped into the gap.

This has not happened in splendid British isolation. Across the Middle East, those who might once have referred to themselves as Arabs increasingly identify themselves as Muslims. The causes are well documented, starting with the failure of alternative movements in those countries, chiefly secular Arab nationalism. The rise of Islamism has also been in step with a surge in fundamentalist movements across the world's major religions. As for its anti-western hue, that is surely, in part, a reaction against decades of outside meddling, particularly in the Middle East. (It's no coincidence that radical Islamism first burst upon the world in Iran, where the west had never stopped trying to run things.) Taken together, it has become an assertive political identity, one that was bound to reverberate throughout the Muslim world, reaching even our own shores.

So this is the wider picture into which the British debate fits. There is a global Islamist movement; some British Muslims choose to identify with it; still more are identified with it by others, whether they like it or not. The result is a degree of suspicion that has thrown petrol on the old "race relations" tensions, which were pretty flammable to start with.

Luckily, this situation is not entirely new for Britain. At the turn of the 20th century, Jews were not only disliked for all the wearily familiar reasons — resentment of the immigrant newcomer and the like — they were also suspected as a disloyal fifth column that was determined to change Britain completely, resorting to violence if necessary. Anarchism and Bolshevism were the feared ideologies of the day, and Jews were said to be bent on bringing them here. Three hundred years earlier, there was similar angst about British Catholics, with their foreign loyalties to Rome and their plans for European domination. Read today's papers warning

'At the turn of the 20th century, Jews were suspected as a disloyal fifth column that was determined to change Britain completely'

of the plot to turn Europe into an Islamic caliphate, and you soon hear the echoes of Britain's past.

How can it be solved? For Catholics, it took the decline of the great Catholic nations of Europe for British Protestantism finally to feel safe, in the 19th century, and to grant basic liberties to those who followed Rome. In the Jewish case, it may be that only the near-destruction of European Jewry by the Nazis beat back British anti-semitism.

But for both Jews and Catholics, it also took time and a defusing of the larger cause with which they were identified by their enemies, or at least some disavowal of the use of force to pursue that cause. Is that what British Muslims need to do now, to allay the fears of their neighbours and distance themselves as clearly as they can from violent Islamism? This is tricky territory: merely to demand such a move puts a pressure on British Muslims that is applied to no other group of citizens. In truth, no one can demand it of that community. If it comes at all, it will have to come from within.

What kind of accommodation with Muslim demands is possible in a multicultural society?
Malieha Malik

Most western liberal democracies are characterised by a deep diversity in terms of race, culture and religion within their populations. Many of the resulting minority groups no longer ask for equality: their most urgent political demands are now for the accommodation of difference. British Muslims who cast their political demands as "accommodate our religion" pose the most acute challenge to liberal democracies. The resulting shift in focus from race to religion, discussed here, challenges the most fundamental beliefs of secular liberals. For this group, the public-private dichotomy is almost an article of faith: they will vigorously defend an individual right to religion in the private sphere while at the same time vigilantly guard the public sphere as a neutral religion-free zone. An international context that ensures coalescence between violence, terrorism and Islam has rendered problematic any sustained analysis of these thorny issues.

"Multiculturalism is the solution" is the response of many thoughtful commentators. It is true that liberal multiculturalism gives minorities an unprecedented opportunity to be equal citizens without suffering the worst excesses of forced assimilation. Multiculturalism is not, however, a panacea. It carries within it a risk of harm to vulnerable individuals within minority communities. Two examples of multicultural accommodation illustrate this point: the first confirms the substantial advantages of making "small concessions"; while the second exposes the risks associated with this process. First, I discuss the benefit of recognising Islamic mortgages, and second, I examine the way in which separate family law tribunals for Muslims can introduce the risk of multicultural vulnerability.

1. Multicultural accommodation: Islamic mortgages

'Family law governs some of the most private and intimate aspects of who we are. It relates to our personal identity in the most profound way'

Islamic law prohibits the charging of interest, making it difficult for Muslims to take out mortgages to buy a home in the UK. In the Finance Act 2003, the government abolished an excessive and double stamp duty on mortgages that comply with the Islamic law. The abolition of this penalty by the Treasury has laid the foundation for cheaper mortgages for Muslims.

These types of modest concessions can yield considerable and magnified political benefits for minorities. Such moves have the potential to reduce the gap between the experiences of Muslims in their daily and practical lives and their experience of mainstream legal and political institutions. This in turn can encourage the meaningful identification of minorities such as British Muslims with mainstream political and legal institutions.

2. Multicultural vulnerability: Muslim women and family law

At first sight the grant of separate jurisdiction to traditional groups in areas of family law seems unproblematic. There is some evidence that some British Muslims would welcome this option. Ontario's Arbitration

Act 1991 allows individuals to resolve civil disputes within their own faith community, providing all affected parties give their consent to the process, and the outcomes respect Canadian law and human rights codes.

Family law governs some of the most private and intimate aspects of who we are. It relates to our personal identity in the most profound way. It therefore seems appropriate to allow citizens in a liberal democracy to reach an agreement about the rules that will govern these aspects of their life. If all persons freely choose to be governed by a traditional justice system, the argument goes, then there seem to be no conclusive reasons why the state should not respect these choices.

This is at first sight an attractive argument, but it overlooks a deeply problematic aspect: the myriad ways in which granting control over family law to a traditional culture or religion has the potential for causing harm to vulnerable group members such as women. It raises the spectre of "multicultural vulnerability" — a term referring to the risk faced by individuals within a minority group whose rights as citizens are compromised by the grant of public recognition to traditional rules and practices. Family law illustrates this vulnerability in its most acute form.

Women and family law become a focus — sometimes an obsession — for traditional groups concerned with the preservation and transmission of their culture or religion because it is women who recreate collective identity through the reproduction and socialising of children. From this perspective, it becomes a critical matter that women should enter into their most intimate relationships and functions in a way that preserves the identity of the whole community. For these reasons the control of women — especially in areas such as sexuality, marriage, divorce and in relation to their children — is a recurring feature of traditional cultural and religious communities. This explains why traditional communities prioritise family law when they make demands for public accommodation.

Crude versions of multiculturalism may suggest that the state should hand over jurisdiction to groups over family law, but a more sophisticated analysis must return to fundamental principles: why are we so concerned with the accommodation of minorities? One of the most powerful arguments for multiculturalism is that there are power hierarchies between minority groups, majorities and the state that should be re-negotiated. However, this recognition of external hierarchies should not blind us to the fact that there are also power hierarchies within groups. Internal inequalities of power may cause vulnerable individuals such as women to bear a disproportionate cost of any policy of accommodation of cultural or religious practices. These costs can include entering into a marriage without the right to divorce; inadequate financial compensation in the case of divorce; giving up the right to custody of children; restriction on the right to education, employment or participation in the public sphere; giving up the right to control over their own reproduction and bodies.

It is often argued that many women choose to remain members of a group despite the fact that traditional rules and practices undermine their interests. "They have a right to exit but they freely choose to remain" is the response to any challenge. But this right-to-exit argument is not a realistic solution to the problem of oppression within groups. It offers an ad hoc and extreme option to what is often a systematic and structural problem within traditional cultures and religions. It puts the burden of resolving these conflicts on individual women and relieves the state (which has conceded jurisdiction in this area to the group) of responsibility for the protection of the fundamental rights of its citizens. Most significantly, the right-to-exit argument suggests that an individual woman at risk from a harmful practice should be the one to abandon her group membership, her family and community. The stark fact is that emotional attachment, economic circumstances and religious commitment makes the "exit" not only an unrealistic, but also a tragic, choice for many Muslim women.

The accommodation of Muslim family law in Britain along the lines developed in Ontario might be possible, but only if we can be sure that the state is able to protect individual women against their communities. There need to be procedures that ensure women are fully informed about the nature and consequences of their choices. There also needs to be more detailed discussion about the limits of individual consent: is there a floor of individual rights that minority women cannot negotiate away? By passing mainstream family law procedures and safeguards in a liberal democracy in favour of traditional forms of justice in special tribunals is a serious decision which deserves sober reflection.

Conclusion

The debate about accommodating British Muslims, and the resulting negotiation between majorities and minorities, needs to be carried out within mainstream political and legal institutions. Civic society and the media are also important actors within this process. This procedure is likely to ensure the broadest range of participation in public debate and political negotiations. In this way the painful compromises that are an inherent part of multicultural politics are more likely to command the consent of all those involved. Points of difference and friction between majorities and minorities can often act as a catalyst towards a stable form of integration that avoids the worst injustices of forced assimilation. In some cases we must be satisfied with an outcome that is a patient and resigned modus vivendi. More optimistically, this technique also has some potential to redeem the worst excesses of multicultural politics: to generate a deeper and more meaningful identification with national institutions for the majority and minority, in a joint enterprise, that creates and sustains a coherent political community. A sense of belonging for all citizens, including British Muslims, can be effectively hammered out through debate and compromise carried out in our public sphere.

Caught between two worlds: how can the state help young Muslims?
Shareefa Fulat

One of the consequences of 9/11 has been to spur a greater political consciousness amongst Muslims. The result is a Muslim faith identity that is often nothing to do with religious practice, and is cultural, political or a reflection of a sense of community.

But what are the consequences of an increasingly assertive Muslim identity on our notions of citizenship and how should a secular state respond to this newly emerging faith identity?

It can be argued that civic engagement and wider public — not just political — participation is crucial to integration. More integration is something that Muslims in Britain seem to be constantly taken to task for in the media and by politicians. Civic engagement can be a powerful tool to aid the process of integration as people from all backgrounds come together over common social needs and concerns that transcend different communities.

In order for individuals and communities to participate and make a contribution to wider public life, they must be able to identify with key public institutions. Nowhere is this more important than the provision of services, which is for most the first point of contact between the citizen and the state.

Muslim communities have the youngest age profile of all faith groups, with 34% under 16 years. Yet in the provision of youth services, there are few if any mainstream and statutory agencies that are able to provide support to Muslim youth which is sensitive to both faith and culture.

The problems faced by Muslim youth are similar to their non-Muslim peers: drugs, mental health, relationships, careers, jobs, training and sexuality. For the Muslim community, however, most of these issues are considered taboo or are largely ignored, making the problems more acute for young Muslims. Any recognition of these issues is largely in the form of chastisement and judgmentalism. In addition, the identity and lifestyle conflicts experienced by many Muslims caught between two worlds may mean that far from providing any support, the family or community are the source of the problem.

'Failure to recognise faith identity means that faith communities are unable to identify with key public institutions'

The experience of the Muslim Youth Helpline shows that young people from Muslim backgrounds are less likely to access mainstream services for fear of being misunderstood. Those that do are less likely to benefit from the support given or follow up on advice or options presented to them.

There is some recognition of this in recent government reports. In March 2003, the National Institute for Mental Health in England report "Inside Out, Improving Mental Health Services for BME Communities in England" identified that NHS plans for mental health "do not adequately address the particular needs of black and minority ethnic groups"; that individuals from BME groups are more at risk of developing mental health problems than majority ethnic groups; that the risk of suicide is higher — particularly among South Asian women — and that cultural conflict is suggested as a factor precipitating suicide in young South Asians.

The report also identified that the voluntary sector has led the development of culturally appropriate services for minority ethnic groups and their effective delivery will be best sustained through partnership between statutory and voluntary service providers, service users and "most importantly BME communities themselves".

The report accepts that statutory agencies acting alone cannot ensure the cultural competency or diversity required by mental health services to meet the needs of BME groups. Mainstream service providers and government should therefore work to build capacity within minority communities.

But the premise behind this kind of report is an acceptance of racial identity — not faith identity. It means that faith-based organisations can find it difficult to qualify for funding and support from statutory agencies.

What secular society doesn't understand is how an increasingly assertive Muslim identity can be a powerful tool to combat traditional taboos of communities which are often mistaken as Islamic oppression. For example, there is no basis in Islam for forced marriages, or so-called honour killings, and the appropriate knowledge of the teachings of Islam are a powerful tool in challenging community attitudes that tolerate such practices to take place. An increasing number of Muslim women are asserting their faith identity and using it as a path to further and higher education.

Without recognition of that faith identity, young Muslims can find themselves caught between a traditional community that views most youth issues as taboo and a mainstream secular society that fails to provide appropriate support.

The consequence of the failure to recognise faith identity is that faith communities are unable to identify with key public institutions and processes and are thereby inadvertently excluded from public life. Nowhere is this more evident than Britain's Muslim communities who are consistently cited as suffering from the worst levels of disadvantage and deprivation according to all socio-economic indicators. This exclusion also forms a barrier to access to services, wider civic engagement and ultimately the process of integration.

In order for Muslims and others from faith communities to engage fully as citizens, there must be recognition of the faith identity in the public sphere. This means more than the provision of information in community languages or halal food; it means engaging Muslim and other faith communities in the delivery of their services and recognising that faith identity has a role to play in British society.

Negotiating new compromises
Geoff Mulgan

Every society and every community rests on a multitude of deals and compromises that help people to live together. Some of these may be very explicit, like the power-sharing arrangements in Lebanon or sex equality legislation. Others may be implicit, like the blind eye that is now turned to prostitution or cannabis use in Britain's big cities to avoid criminalising large swathes of the population. When large numbers of people feel that these deals are unfair, the result is usually instability or worse. When most of the people feel that they are broadly fair, societies get by.

Britain has now been through roughly half a century of trying to work out the deals appropriate for a growing population of migrants and minorities. Most of the time it has been pragmatic: less dogmatic than France; less assertive on assimilation than much of northern Europe; and reasonably flexible on a multitude of practical issues ranging from halal food to providing prayer facilities or finding alternatives to alcohol-based products to preserve dead bodies.

In the 70s and 80s the primary concern for policy-makers was to encourage tolerance and discourage overt racism, through a combination of positive policies to promote multiculturalism and legal moves to ban discrimination and incitement to hatred. However, as many societies have discovered, tolerance is rarely a sufficient answer. Societies only work because some things are not tolerated, such as racist violence or female circumcision (heroin use and fox-hunting are more complex examples). Indeed, you could say that any society defines what it values through the things it doesn't tolerate as well as the things that it does; human rights have become a foundation stone defining the non-negotiable limits for many societies, including Britain. Multiculturalism was a healthy corrective to monoculturalism, but proved by no means sufficient in helping diverse communities to live together; partly because it failed to answer where the limits should be defined, and partly because it gave insufficient guidance as to how to strike the thousands of big and small deals that help a society to get by.

Striking these deals has proved particularly important, and difficult, in relation to Islam. As Sunder Katwala shows, Islam is much more self-conscious about the public nature of religion than Christianity. Attempts at compromise have increasingly been overshadowed by the sincerely held belief of millions of people that a war is now under way between Islam and the west. They include belligerent American Christian Republicans, secular European liberals who see Islam as uniquely intolerant, violent and dogmatic (and Turkey as a mortal threat to the EU), and Islamic activists who interpret every event from Chechnya to Iraq as further evidence of a western conspiracy to destroy Islam. They also include the activists who threatened voters in Bethnal Green before the 2005 election on the grounds that voting is un-Islamic.

Getting these compromises right is also difficult because for Britain's

1.6 million Muslims any generalisations are deceptive. Lumping together wealthy Arabs in west London, poor Punjabis in Birmingham, Bangladeshis from rural Sylhet in Tower Hamlets and middle-class Indian Muslims in Leicester, can obscure more than it illuminates, and many familiar problems (such as high unemployment, poor housing and discrimination) are now mixed in with many less familiar advances (for example in school results or political clout). So while it is true, for example, that more British Muslims now define themselves as Muslim first, rather than as Turks or Bengalis or Arabs, this is by no means a universal pattern.

> **'Conflicts are never caused or resolved in any simple way by identity, culture or economics'**

As Britain tries to find a distinctive set of deals around which communities can coexist and intermingle, history provides some grounds for hope. A hundred and eighty years ago, England's Catholics were widely seen as a fifth column. They were allied to our historic enemy (and France was a far more serous threat than al-Qaida will ever be). They answered to a foreign Pope and, as the public were constantly reminded by ranting Protestant priests, Catholicism threatened our most cherished values of liberty and democracy. Yet the clash of civilisations never happened. Within a few decades Catholics were being successfully integrated. The worst legal discrimination had been removed and the earlier anxieties had come to seem faintly absurd. More recent history confirms the point. In the 70s and 80s Irish migrants to Britain found themselves on the receiving end of public distrust and sometimes harassment from the police who suspected them of sympathy for the IRA (and of course many pubs in places such as Kilburn were fundraising targets for the IRA at the same time as other pubs were targets for their bombs). Twenty years later these fears have almost entirely disappeared and the traffic in casual labour has reversed, as British builders cross over to the higher wages available in Dublin.

This example confirms the wider lesson of history. Conflicts are never caused or resolved in any simple way by identity, culture or economics. Where resources are scarce, or there are strong historical memories of conflict, small events are more likely to inflame passions. But all over the world many communities that might be expected to be divided live happily together, just as many communities that were previously integrated (as in Yugoslavia, India or Rwanda) have descended into bitter hatreds.

What makes the difference? Dealing with underlying structural problems helps, but not as much as how people and institutions behave: whether communities turn a blind eye to provocations; whether intellectuals and journalists allow lies to take root; whether leaders whip small resentments into big ones; whether states respond with sensitivity or crude force.

For Britain, three conclusions follow. First, leaders and institutions need to take great care over what they say and do, whether they are mullahs or ministers. Such things as wrongful arrests can have a disproportionate impact. Responsible leadership in a diverse society has to mean thinking through all of the possible effects of words and actions.

Second, we need to fight the myths on all sides. Secular commentators should be challenged when they claim that Islam is uniquely violent: what about the horrors committed in the name of Christianity, secular communism or for that matter Hinduism? They should be challenged when they paint Islam as uniquely intolerant: what of the Emperor Akbar who remains the world's best example of active rather than passive tolerance? Or as bound to subordinate civil life to religion: what about Turkish or for that matter Ottoman history?

Equally, Salafi extremists operating within Muslim communities should be challenged when they propagate lies about American or Zionist conspiracies, and when they exploit real grievances over Palestine but ignore the complexities of Kosovo or Bosnia (when the west came to the aid of a Muslim minority being oppressed by a Christian majority), or the inconvenient fact that the worst slaughter of Muslims of recent years (in the Iran/Iraq war) was at the hands of other Muslims. It is as unacceptable for commentators to paint any critic of Islam as an Islamophobe, as it is for secular writers to denounce all advocates of distinctively Islamic solutions as archaic anachronisms.

Third, we need new deals to be negotiated, compromises that allow life to go on, and to hold resentments at bay. Some of those implicit deals are already taking shape. As Maleiha Malik shows, the picture is complex and quite fluid: small compromises on Islamic mortgages removed an implicit discrimination against Muslims, but any introduction of Islamic law into family life may run counter to women's legitimate rights. In other areas, too, the deals are likely to be complex. So autonomy to run Islamic schools can be balanced with a commitment to the national curriculum so that children are prepared for life in modern Britain, and with more chances for young Muslims (and their often equally isolated white working-class counterparts) to mix with others. Some of these deals may be uncomfortable when they touch on such issues as the non-negotiability of free speech, the possibility of a limited role for sharia law, or a stronger emphasis on English-language skills. Atheists need to work harder at understanding what it feels like to see religion as something more than a private preference (and why some Muslims experience liberal criticisms as an attack on their identity, not just their ideas); equally believers need to appreciate that they are living in what is now an overwhelmingly secular society.

All of these issues have to be talked about and negotiated politically, not treated as matters of absolute and immovable principle. Societies can easily talk themselves into conflict and misery. But they can also talk, and act, their way out.

Part 3
Habits of solidarity: the politics of living together

Questions of race and identity are clouding the more important issue of how to improve the everyday lives of British Muslims

Sukhvinder Stubbs

The 2005 election was a vivid reminder of the fact that the Muslim voters are becoming both significant and distinctive. Unlike whites or other minority ethnic groups, Muslims list issues of religious symbolism as their highest priority. Relatively little regard is given by Muslim communities, Pakistanis and Bangladeshis in particular, to their local conditions. Community effort is instead applied to secure national and international standards that reinforce collective religious identity.

Take, for example, the legislation to counter incitement to religious hatred. While this was one of the recommendations that I was involved in formulating as part of the Commission on British Muslims and Islamophobia back in 1997 and I am pleased to see the bill being debated in parliament, yet I found myself astonished to see it become the focus of such a huge community response. The same report contained numerous other recommendations, many relating to local issues of poverty and disadvantage that remain unfulfilled. Likewise, it is understandable that in the climate since 9/11, many Muslims have taken an intense interest in the Iraq conflict, with anti-war feelings running high. However, I was surprised to read an ICM poll in 2003 which highlighted that more Muslims were concerned about the dispute in Kashmir than the education of their children or their health.

However, this high level of engagement with the political process, which leaders repeatedly assure us is the only way to have a stake in any future social improvements, has signally failed to deliver on the bread-and-butter issues for Muslims. Even left-leaning people find it hard to explain away in sociological terms why poverty should be so entrenched in these communities. Considered alongside the social mobility of other South Asian groups, that of Pakistanis and Bangladeshis appears sluggish. Adherence to traditional dress is viewed as part of the stubborn unwillingness to move on. Difficulties in speaking English, even among younger generations and sustained strong links with their villages of origin reinforce a perception that they don't belong to our society. Political correctness is believed to forbid any reasonable discussion of these problems. As a result, there is an unspoken sense that they are a burden on society and indigenous folk, a feeling fostered by many who consider themselves moderate and sensible in outlook, a feeling picked up on and exploited by the far right. Pakistani and Bangladeshi communities are considered a threat to cohesion and integration. This is despite evidence that the disturbances in the northern towns were stoked by the BNP.

Responsibility for the relative lack of attention given to such basic concerns in the Muslim community is widespread, ranging from establishment politicians and local authorities to community and religious leaders who may not always best represent the interests of their people. As for ordinary Muslims themselves, the fairly simple, rural background of most Pakistanis and Bangladeshis is often used to explain their lack of complaint for their lot. While this is honourable and true to an extent, it

'You know that the Muslim vote counts when the Labour party treat Blackburn as a highly vulnerable marginal seat to be defended at all costs' would apply equally to many Sikh communities too, who nonetheless tend to do well economically. The modesty that comes with Islamic faith, gentleness, lack of ostentation and concern for the common Muslim good or *ummah* may be more relevant. Antipathy with most forms of capitalism has also been used to justify an entrepreneurially more passive stance. Furthermore, the edict in the Qur'an that forbids paying or receiving interest, known as *riba*, explains low levels of home ownership. Even this, though, doesn't fully set out why certain Muslim communities haven't kept pace with other minority ethnic groups.

It is particularly hard to explain away the deprivation and disadvantage suffered by Pakistanis and Bangladeshis given their relatively high level of engagement with politics. You might have thought that long-standing links with the Labour party would, by now, have paid some social dividend. Many veteran Labour MPs holding seats with rapidly growing Muslim constituents have relied on their support. There are 41 constituencies where Muslims comprise more than 10% of the population and at least 10 where they make up between 20%–50%. Furthermore, they are more likely to vote than their white peers. Overall, there are in the region of a 100 constituencies where the Muslim vote could hold sway. Sher Khan from the Muslim Council of Britain states that the Muslim community is now the most politicised it has ever been.

The last election revealed the level of potential power wielded. You know that the Muslim vote counts when the Labour party treat Blackburn as a highly vulnerable marginal seat to be defended at all costs. Its MP, Jack Straw, breathed a huge sigh of relief at maintaining a much reduced majority. Blackburn has around 27,000 Muslims and Jack Straw had a majority of a little over 9,000. It's just as well for him that he had no serious opponent, otherwise he might have been in greater trouble. Other seemingly unassailable Labour seats that took huge knocks include Manchester Gorton (Gerald Kaufman lost nearly 11% to the Liberals), Bradford North (Terry Rooney suffered a 10% swing to the Liberals) and Hornsey and Wood Green (where Barbara Roche was unseated by a massive 14.6% swing). More spectacular, though less well recognised than George Galloway's maverick success in Bethnal Green, was Salma Yaqoob of Respect, who forced a swing of 21% against Labour in Sparkbrook.

Although high levels of political engagement and relative clout are a good thing, they become problematic in the context of continued high levels of deprivation. In practice this probably stokes a feeling, as well as the actuality, of marginalisation. Equally sad, however, is that a similar obsession over identity, this time an assumed sense of Englishness, fuels many very badly off whites, who blame their situation on a host of equally unfortunate "theys", from Muslims to asylum seekers, whom they regard as unjustly favoured competitors for resources. Whites and Muslims actually have a great deal in common. Both are inclined towards a sense of pride: a source of comfort but also of being under siege. Both face material disadvantage and are lagging behind other ethnic groups. Both face the sort of social problems that tend to arise, especially among young people (drug abuse, anti-social behaviour), from poor upbringings, Muslims no less so than whites, despite religious constrictions.

Madeleine Bunting has called for greater emphasis on developing "habits of solidarity". Nowhere is this potential more evident than among working-class whites and Muslims. Yet they remain divided, not just in

'To redress the lot of Muslims in the UK will require some serious re-thinking, re-education and imagination'

the northern towns where segregation is so visible, but in numerous other boroughs across the country where deep schisms exist between Muslim and white communities. Where political masters barely understand either community, it is not surprising that they might prefer to keep them apart. Pioneers such as Ted Cantle are making efforts to reconcile difference and build on mutual interest. But the "pancakes and poppadums" approach to community cohesion is a superficial response to groups of people with such deep-seated values. What is needed is a form of reconciliation and mediation that draws out common human, emotional and physical needs.

To redress the lot of Muslims in the UK will require some serious re-thinking, re-education and imagination on the part of everyone from government and policymakers to community and religious leaders, to ordinary Muslims and ordinary white people. At the moment, too much policy is based on the assumption that the inherent problems of Muslim-ness inhibit their proper integration into society. This may be intended as delicate policymaking but only exacerbates an unhelpful sense of the supposed otherness and difference of Muslims. It's time to move away from these questions of race, identity and "what it is to be British" and square up to the practical, secular questions of how to improve the every-day lives of poor Muslims.

A Community in crisis
Tahir Abbas and Phoebe Griffith

There are now 1.6 million Muslims in the UK, and over 80% live in the five major conurbations of Greater London, West Midlands, West Yorkshire, Greater Manchester and East Midlands. The largest community of Muslims — over 40% of the total — is in London. Around 1 million originate from South Asia and of them, three-quarters come from Pakistan, and the remainder from Bangladesh and India. Another 600,000 come from a huge range of countries including Afghanistan, Iran, Turkey, Kurdistan, Serbia, North Africa and Somalia.

More than two-thirds of Muslims live below the poverty line in the UK. This is partly due to the fact that the employment rates for Pakistani and Bangladeshi men are so low: one in five are out of work, which is almost double the rate for African Caribbeans and three times that for Indians. In 2000, despite an unprecedentedly tight labour market, the chances of ethnic minorities not having a job were still higher than for whites 10 years previously at a time of much higher unemployment.

Another key factor is that Muslims are disproportionately clustered in low-paid work, which explains the high rates of means-tested state benefit: they are the most dependent group living in the UK today with two-fifths of Muslim couples with at least one adult in employment receiving some sort of means tested support — five times the rate of whites. While Indian Hindus are over-represented in the medical and accountancy sectors, for example one-third of Bangladeshi men work as cooks or waiters. Many workers have turned to these jobs because they found themselves trapped in declining sectors, such as clothing and textiles.

The poverty impacts on Muslims' access to decent housing: 42% live in overcrowded accommodation, compared with 12% of the general population. Twelve per cent of Muslim children live in households without central heating, twice the number of all dependent children. Poor quality housing and low income have obvious consequences for health, with Muslims suffering disproportionately from a variety of illnesses, including heart disease and diabetes.

Muslim communities have remained concentrated in the inner city areas of older towns and cities in the north, the Midlands, and the south. It is an indicator of how they have not benefited from the levels of mobility enjoyed by other migrant communities, and of their inability to move out of areas that are facing high levels of social tension and economic deprivation. Birmingham is typical of many of the challenges faced by Muslims across the country. Roughly one in seven of the city's inhabitants are Muslim and their unemployment rate is three times that of the overall city levels.

The experience of Birmingham's Muslims brings into focus the fact that economic opportunities have tended to bypass Muslim communities, even when other communities have prospered. While other cities with large Muslim populations, such as Bradford, are trapped in economic decay, overall Birmingham's economic performance has been good,

'Twelve per cent of Muslim children live in houses without central heating, twice the number of all dependent children'

despite the decline of its manufacturing and engineering sectors. The city has undergone successful regeneration and this has attracted a thriving service and commercial sector. Nevertheless, these opportunities have largely bypassed most Muslims and may have even entrenched some of the barriers which they face. While the indigenous population has moved out of inner city Birmingham through "white flight", South Asian Muslims have failed to move beyond the inner city areas to which they originally migrated. Subsequently, these areas have become further disadvantaged with new employment created elsewhere.

As is the case with all communities, the performance of Muslim children in the UK holds the key to tackling poverty in the future. It is particularly important in view of the fact that one-third of all British Muslims are under the age of 14. However, the figures for achievement are as bleak as those relating to the labour market. Sixty-nine per cent of all Muslim children are living in poverty and, as such, they are exposed to a wide range of risk factors: overcrowded accommodation, inadequate housing and the fact that carers are likely to be unemployed, be very low paid, or are having to bring up children alone (19%).

Because a high proportion of Muslim fathers lack formal education and work as semi-skilled manual workers, they don't have the tools to ensure that their children are being properly served by the education system, even when, as research shows, Muslim parents do aspire for their children to achieve higher levels of education. Role models are also lacking, as most adult Muslim women do not have paid employment outside the home and older siblings will tend to be unemployed. Only 11% of Pakistani women and only 4% of Bangladeshi women are in full-time employment.

Inevitably, Muslims' children are served by worse schools because they live in less well off neighbourhoods. Furthermore, they are handicapped by higher levels of prejudice which tends to affect the level of care they receive within the education system. For example, qualitative studies have found that teachers tend to view the problems facing their Muslim pupils exclusively in cultural terms and will commonly identify "excessive in-marrying" or "a lack of desire to integrate" as the drivers for the underachievement of their Muslims pupils. As a result, many fail to identify the structural issues which may affect the children's performance in the classroom. It is hardly surprising then that Muslim children underperform in the education system, with only 40% achieving five GCSE passes, against 64% and 73% of Indian and Chinese respectively. Shockingly, 36% of all British Muslim children are leaving school with no qualifications at all and one-fifth of 16- to 24-year-old Muslims are unemployed.

Although government policy aimed at improving the life chances of the most disadvantaged should have a significant impact on Muslims, current poverty alleviation strategies are not tailored to meet the needs of Muslims. For example, anti-poverty strategies rely heavily on getting women into work. But such strategies fail to address the reluctance for women to work within the Pakistani and Bangladeshi communities either because of lack of skills, opportunities or because of unwillingness for women with family responsibilities to work outside the home. Muslim women have the lowest employment rate of any group in the UK labour market.

But there is also another problem about the government's current anti-poverty strategy. Despite the mounting evidence of their deprivation,

'36% of all British Muslim children are leaving school with no qualifications at all and one-fifth of 16- to 24-year-old Muslims are unemployed'

Muslims are still not identified as a target when it comes to disadvantaged groups. There are significant gaps in the collection of data according to faith — data continues to be collected according to ethnicity — particularly in the key area of education.

Finally, discrimination is inevitably impacting on the willingness of Muslims to engage with government policy. Studies by the Open Society Institute have revealed that ethnic Muslims face the highest levels of discrimination in key areas, including the labour market and in the criminal justice system. Surveys show that job candidates with Muslim names arc thc least likely to secure interviews, and there is evidence to demonstrate that Muslims are among the most likely targets of stop and search operations since the introduction of anti-terrorism legislation. But the most disturbing evidence of an increasing Muslim alienation from the state is in their low levels of trust in the police and the criminal justice system. Muslims are more likely than other ethnic groups to be victims of crime, including racially motivated crime. They also have the lowest satisfaction levels with public-initiated police contact and the lowest levels of confidence in the police. Unlike in other public services, Muslims who have had contact with the Crown Prosecution Service, the Prison Service and the Probation Service are more likely to feel they will be discriminated against than those who have not had contact with these services. Muslims make up 3% of the UK population but 9% of the population of prisoners.

It is not a surprise then that Muslims have low levels of engagement when it comes to state-driven initiatives, and reflect the greatest tendency to meet their needs through self-sufficiency, a strategy that has so far proved ineffective and is unlikely to significantly improve the position of the Muslim community. At the same time, the rise of certain trends of separatism and extremism among some sections of the community could further increase the marginalisation of Muslims, and contribute to even more tension. In the context of growing global instability and higher levels of distrust, failure to address the barriers faced by Muslims will lead to a serious deterioration in community relations.

England: a segregated country?
Ted Cantle

Since the second world war, the many forms of segregation and separation of white, black and ethnic minority communities have been reinforced, rather than broken down. The possibilities for interaction have been sharply restricted by the patterns of settlement across the UK. Britain may be a multicultural society but most of the British do not live in a multicultural community. In 1961 London contained 47% of the UK's black and ethnic minority population and the West Midlands conurbation 14%. Some 40 years later the figures are almost exactly the same. It is simply not possible to promote respect and understanding between different cultures when the lack of contact prevents the development of any real knowledge or understanding.

Oona King MP described to her colleagues in parliament her sense of shock at finding segregated schools in her London constituency: "I have mentioned before in parliament my shock at visiting two schools next door to each other soon after I was elected in 1997. They shared a playground with a fence down the middle. On one side of the fence there were white children playing with a smattering of Afro-Caribbeans and on the other there were brown, Muslim and Bangladeshi children. Perhaps it is because my father was brought up in the segregated south that I was horrified by that; I could not believe it. We read about such things, but when we see them in Britain, we must think that something is seriously wrong."

Most of the ethnic minority population live in London and a few other large towns and cities, while the white population dominates most of the rest of the country, with areas such as the north-east, Wales and the south-west being almost exclusively white. Even in areas that are more mixed, the separation is often just as evident, with most towns and cities divided on a neighbourhood basis.

The term "segregation" is often used to describe this separation, but it is not really appropriate. Segregation literally implies divisions that are imposed and enforced by regulation. Clearly there is no such regime in force and it is therefore assumed that "self-segregation", in which some people prefer to live in an area dominated by their own ethnic or faith group, is much the same thing. However, in reality, choices of where to live are often constrained by socio-economic factors, the lack of appropriate social and cultural facilities, the location of suitable schools and, most of all, by real concerns about the lack of safety and security in other areas.

Some ethnic minority households have, of course, had the necessary resources and confidence to move out of their traditional area, but such movement is still limited and is counteracted by the "white flight", in which white families move out of mixed areas, sometimes in pursuit of what they see as better housing or schools, or because they are afraid that their present area will "tip over" into a predominantly black area and that this is somehow less desirable. The net result is the growth of even more obvious divisions between majority and minority ethnic groups.

Many of these "segregated" communities are so dominated by particular groups that the possibility of contact with the majority population or another minority group is very limited. These "parallel lives" do not meet at any point, with little or no opportunity to explore the differences and to build mutual respect, let alone to see them as enriching our communities. Meanwhile, racists can easily spread myths and false rumours and use this ignorance of each other to demonise minorities.

That is not to say that we should attempt to go in the opposite direction towards some form of total integration or "assimilation". Some degree of "clustering" for each group is essential if we are serious about preserving cultural identity. A critical mass of each community will also be necessary to support different places of worship, shops and social facilities. But little thought is being given to the future form that neighbourhoods should adopt and there are few techniques available to help to shape them. Indeed, little is currently being done to understand and map community dynamics and to try to assist mixed developments and the consequent interaction that different forms help to facilitate. By and large, existing settlement patterns — and the segregation and separation they create — are being reinforced and perpetuated.

This is evident in the present pattern of migration and, alarmingly, the consequences seem not to have been considered in relation to new developments. The Office of the Deputy Prime Minister's proposals for the building of 500,000 new homes in the south-east, under the somewhat dubious title of "sustainable communities", makes no mention of community cohesion and neither does the parallel proposal for the north — "The Northern Way".

These huge projects propose to build a number of entirely new small towns. But it seems likely that this once-in-a-generation opportunity to build communities that are accessible and desirable to a wide range of people from different backgrounds may be lost. For example, the Bangladeshi community is currently locked into Tower Hamlets by a mixture of structural barriers such as high house prices, the location of cultural facilities and concerns about security and safety; who is thinking about what it would take to ensure they could find the Thames Gateway attractive? Or, could the Thames Gateway, instead, exacerbate the white flight from the existing mixed areas and reinforce ethnic concentrations in inner city London?

We still fail to put a premium on interaction, but how can we possibly expect people to develop any form of relationship unless they can have the opportunity to build an understanding of each other? If they continue to live "parallel lives" with no meaningful contact at any point, the ignorance will grow into suspicion and fear. Proximity between different groups is not, in itself, enough. It may lead to contact in many different aspects of daily life; for example, mixed school classes and the informal friendships formed at the school gate, the participation in local sports and cultural events and joint training. But it should not be taken for granted that proximity leads to interaction; even the most benign activities can become segregated — remember the recent Commission for Racial Equality's survey finding that "95% of whites had no black friends". Confidence building has to take place on both sides and relationships have to be built in non-threatening ways; for example, there are now many school-twinning arrangements that allow all-black and

'Existing settlement patterns — and the segregation and separation which they create — are being reinforced and perpetuated'

all-white schools to undertake joint curricular and extra-curricular activities as a prelude to mixed intakes.

There are real practical difficulties to overcome, too, especially for the many white children growing up in all-white parts of the country, who have no experience of the multicultural society of which they are a part. Many do not meet people from black and ethnic minority backgrounds until they go to university — and university is still an option for only a minority of youngsters. Policies to promote community cohesion will have to be shaped to reach them, too; for example, the way in which Wigan, a largely white area, has teamed-up some of its schools with youngsters in multicultural Leicester.

But it is not just about sharing experiences, it is also about sharing a vision and sense of purpose. We need a more positive approach to breaking down segregation and "parallel lives" and ensuring that people interact and develop mutual understanding. This means not only interacting in our daily lives, but also as part of a political entity, as nationals with a common interest in the direction and development of the state. If not, we will forever be attempting to micro-manage behaviour through ever more increasing legislation to prevent discrimination and ensure equal opportunities, rather than changing underlying attitudes and values and making the changes self-sustaining.

Interaction – where is it happening? Who shapes it and who promotes it?
Indra Adnan

The Bradford riots of 2001 marked a watershed for race relations in the UK. It led to Ted Cantle's now celebrated phrase "parallel lives". In his review of the riots and, as he explained more fully in his subsequent Social Cohesion Review for the Home Office, there is a danger of fragmentation when we focus on the "right to be different": "'ethnic groups'... retreat into comfort zones, made up of people like themselves". It was an implicit critique of a form of multiculturalism that emphasises difference and was a signal for more pluralistic approaches within an overarching goal of cohesion and participation.

The shift of direction has prompted a proliferation of public service initiatives to promote these goals. Leicester city council was awarded Beacon status for its broad response to the theme. It launched a host of initiatives targeted at neighbourhood regeneration, as well as spending £3m on creative partnership events in the fields of sports, arts, fashion and architecture. Twinning schools has proved a popular council strategy, as well as working through tenants associations to "mix up" segregated communities. Policy officer Monica Glover said: "People want to live together in their cultural groups and lead parallel lives. But when these segregated communities score high on the deprivation indices, and qualify for extra grants and subsidies, the wider community sees that as to do with their ethnicity and it causes tension."

Glover feels that Leicester values its diversity, but believes this approach is not a barrier to cohesion. "Cultural identity is fluid and changes over time — it is not monolithic."

At Bradford Vision, Pam Hardisty, director of neighbourhood renewal, draws attention to a number of innovative micro ideas. For example, 20% of the annual budget for realising the government goals of participation is given directly to the community to allocate. Small groups of people formulate an idea of how they would spend the money. Each group gets five minutes to talk about their idea, and the community chooses the best. What is remarkable, says Hardisty, is that voting does not take place along the traditional race or even neighbourhood lines. People tend to go for the group that shows most passion and commitment.

Some of the most vital and challenging developments are coming from youth projects. One popular initiative has been the youth parliaments (YP) — with the election of national and local youth MPs to discuss issues, make recommendations to local councils and encourage participation in community life. Greg Spencer, administrator of the Bradford Keighley YP, described the group of 30 as "totally mixed".

They voted racism the fourth most important issue to tackle — below drugs and guns, bullying and youth provisions. "With young people you have to keep cool. You go into clubs and do workshops about drugs and you don't talk about what colour they are unless they want to," says Spencer. It can stir up controversy, however: young people copy each others' styles and ideas, and discuss their beliefs; it can provoke fear

> 'Cultural identity is fluid and changes over time – it is not monolithic'

about fusion and hybridity.

Original ideas for creating new cross-cultural meeting grounds are also emerging from the private sector. Unltd is a social entrepreneur fund that provides small and medium grants for start-ups; for example, Jan Smithies' Spice! project; a visitor centre in Bradford celebrating different cultures through "food, scents, textiles and colours"; Isabel Carlisle's Festival of Muslim Cultures project is another.

But the whole policy of cohesion raises issues of how far and how much integration communities want. Leicester city council tells of its successfully integrated but culturally separate Muslim youth. Paul Winstone, policy officer for race relations, says there is "No clubbing, drinking or dating: they're proud of their difference and everyone respects that. Some of our most important work — such as the creation of Islamic burial services and the exploration into Islamic banking — is not just tolerating, but respecting, real difference."

Is it helpful, furthermore, to keep addressing cohesion as a problem of ethnic minorities? As Bradford's Pam Hardisty says: "There are still the problems of the poor white communities. No one holds much information about young white men — they just sign on and take part in an alternative economy, disconnected from the mainstream. Who, except the BNP, asks them who they want to be?"

Bano Murtuja, who together with Tom Wakeford has been running citizens' juries in the North of England, says: "The government's policy on cohesion is not engaging enough people. It comes across as authoritarian: you will be a stakeholder in your society, in a prescribed number of ways, whether you want to or not. If not — or if you don't know what you want — where can you go for more open dialogue without prescribed ends?"

Citizens' juries are a mixed panel of usually 12 people, self-selecting from a larger group drawn at random from the electoral roll. They come together to explore issues they choose, at their own pace and with their own agenda. In contrast to the legal model of jury practice, they are given time to deliberate freely with each other and interrogate the witnesses themselves. Their conclusions, importantly, need not be unanimous. "Imagine," says Murtuja, "everyone feels they have a right to be heard: Citizens' juries gives those people that access.

"In Blackburn, there were participants who had never spoken to an Asian before. Yet their issues generally cut across the racial divide — young people, drink and drugs, then immigration — in that order. People need to be heard on the same subjects that the BNP will try to raise. On the whole, this isn't an "us and them" problem: engagement is subtle and nuanced. We're not talking about race."

Another attempt to have more open-ended dialogue was called Building Good Relations in Oldham, a new partnership between the voluntary groups, including inter-faith, and the statutory bodies — police, social services and health — in the area. In a bold move, they invited Brendan MacAllister from Mediation Northern Ireland to share his experience of conflict resolution work in Belfast and apply the learning to local problems.

"There are four essential aspects to peace-building," says MacAllister. "First, the capacity to imagine the centrality of relationships. Second, that individuals develop the trust to transcend the gap between their world and others, but, in so doing, remain authentic. Third, a belief in creativity rather than over-reliance on technique. Fourth, a willingness to walk into unknown spaces without a map."

'The important task is to create spaces in which a "safe" dialogue can take place. People want to talk but are afraid of getting it wrong'

Craig Russell, head of the diversity and cohesion unit in Oldham metropolitan and borough council, described the process: "Conflict resolution training helped us to understand that it's not just physics — working with the systems of representation, planning the schedule — but chemistry. You need to work on the right mix of people in the dialogue at any time: people with different levels of commitment — some sure, some less convinced of the value of multiculturalism or cohesion. Although we worked through recognised voluntary groups, it was not the usual representatives who took part. People with more diverse views got involved."

MacAllister says: "Community cohesion will be slow, unless a way is found to liberate the community from the constraints of government process. Public services should concentrate on mediation, contributing to, but not resolving conflicts. Mediation assists in communication and supporting creative thinking. It is the protagonists... that have to agree to what they can live with."

Some of the most important opportunities for interaction are being facilitated by Muslims. The City Circle — groups of Muslim business men and women hosting mixed forums for open discussion — are operating in London, Birmingham and Reading. They have also established out-of-school learning clubs and projects for the homeless; they aim to promote an understanding of Islam as philanthropic. New Muslim media — Q-News, the innumerable Muslim blogs on the internet — are also great displays of a very broad and eclectic debate taking place outside of government-designated areas.

Whether cohesion is the correct target for our multicultural society or not, some patience is clearly required, as many of these initiatives are new and faltering. As Bradford's Pam Hardisty says: "The important task is to create spaces in which a 'safe' dialogue can take place. People want to talk but are afraid of getting it wrong. Our role is to facilitate this dialogue and to support people through what is still a very new process."

We have to be honest about the problems in the Muslim community

Ann Cryer MP

Published
21/01/05
The Guardian

Keighley is an industrious, innovative and thriving town. A centre of excellence in engineering, a world-renowned tourist industry and fast becoming the residentially desirable suburb for the expanding metropolis of Leeds and Bradford.

The town has everything going for it. However, because of the actions of a minority, treading on eggshells is a rough summary of the situation I find myself in as the MP for Keighley. Since the leader of the British National Party announced earlier this year his decision to contest the parliamentary seat at the general election, I am left cogitating on whether I can carry on with campaigns against forced marriages; for more marriages within the settled community; greater use of English in Bangladeshi and Pakistani homes; encouraging more Asian people (especially women) to become involved in public life rather than relying on unelected representatives; supporting the employment of Imams educated at UK Islamic colleges rather than those trained exclusively on the sub-continent; and further challenges to the ill-treatment of children in some madrassas.

The Pakistani and Bangladeshi communities of towns like Keighley can continue to marry first cousins from the subcontinent and sponsor their entry to the UK as a spouse, but the result for most and for their community is the economic and social underachievement that has regrettably become the norm. Therefore, I must continue my campaigns for the protection and betterment of the most vulnerable in those two communities, but clearly my role in these areas is going to be increasingly fraught given that the extremists of the BNP will make the most negative and racist political capital of such issues.

There are sections of the white community in Keighley that have been unhelpful in engineering the right atmosphere to find humanitarian solutions to problems. Consider, for example, residents of a village organising such a campaign of vilification against a proposed home for eight children in care that social services had to drop the idea. Consider an angry meeting a few weeks ago, rapidly convened to oppose planning permission for a new refuge for women and children fleeing domestic violence. Possibly even worse is the story of white children being withdrawn by parents from classes designed to discuss Islam — only one a week for six weeks, but apparently too much for some Keighleians.

I have always realised that one of the unfortunate by-products of daring to discuss controversial issues such as race, social cohesion or immigration is the room it gives to extremist pressure groups to hijack the debate. However, it is important to appreciate that this is a reflex action by the extremists who have a political interest in ensuring that no one touch on these subjects in a rational, humane — although probing — way. Their raison d'etre is to allow such issues to fester. Discussion, debate and positive resolution would take away the extremists' very source of energy. However, shying away — in fear of potential repercussions and the reaction of extremists — would be tantamount to doing the extremists' bidding.

In Keighley, like many other northern towns and cities, it is the appeasement of unacceptable behaviour, excused by "traditional values", that has no place in a modern society, and which has created the environment that has allowed extremist politics to take root.

For the sake of the honest, decent and hardworking majority of the people I represent, I will not tailor my politics to conform to white or Asian intolerance or the extremist policies of the BNP.

Attempts to Anglicise Muslims will only backfire

Azhar Hussain

The first generation of immigrants were attracted to Keighley by the plenitude of jobs available in the then thriving textile industry. This proud generation of Pakistanis who witnessed the birth of their nation were never willing to lose their identity as Pakistanis. They lived in the hope that they would, one day, return home. Some realised their hopes in their lifetimes; the majority of the rest ensured that at least their mortal remains returned to be buried in the motherland.

The second generation, most of whom are now in their 50s, never entertained hopes of resettling in Pakistan, yet they are equally passionate about their Pakistani identity. However, at the same time they have developed an affiliation with Keighley of which they are proud. Keighley is just as much home as the village back in Pakistan — hence they move frequently, between the two.

It takes time for new identities to form and mature, just as it takes time for inherited identities to fade. Keighley's Muslims have always been aware that, with time, the deep-rooted identity with Pakistan would gradually weaken. They have never opposed this; what they object to is the sudden severing of all ties with Pakistan and its cultural heritage. That younger generations are more Keighlian than Pakistani has been seen as both inevitable and positive.

While aspects of our Pakistani identity may fade, the most important source of our complex identity is Islam, our religion. While we can tolerate restrictions of our Pakistani identity, we cannot compromise on religious issues. This sentiment is shared with almost all sections of the Muslim community.

Interestingly, Pakistani Muslims often identify themselves as Keighlians rather than British or English. It is the local not the national identity that is meaningful. Many Muslims today would be offended if they were told that their white neighbours were more Keighlian than they were. But affiliation to national identity is weak; people of my generation wouldn't take on conspicuous symbols such as wearing an English football shirt or displaying English flags. However, I think that will change and I expect an English identity to grow rapidly among future generations. Already, the young children of the fourth generation are seen running around in England shirts.

The growth in English identity among Pakistani Muslims must be organic. Outside attempts to Anglicise this proud community, or to deny and resist the existence of complex identities will only backfire. Within the community, members must allow each other to move at their own pace. Those who prefer a slower pace cannot be labelled "uncompromising", while others should not be termed "coconuts" for moving quicker.

But there are two questions that crop up repeatedly over how the Muslim community in Keighley is evolving.

First, why is the Muslim community so highly segregated? Some may argue that this is proof that Muslims are unwilling or unable to intermingle. Others insist transcontinental marriages are to blame. I believe that this unhealthy ghettoising, although inevitable in early generations, is changing with a younger generation — but to what extent they will succeed remains to be seen.

We moved to our current home 15 years ago, becoming one of three Muslim families living in a street of 20 houses. Within a couple of years, almost all the white neighbours had fled.

Currently, my family and I are in the process of relocating into a white middle-class residential area. Many Muslim families have already preceded us; but what worries me is that there are signs that existing white residents maybe fleeing again. This would be a disaster since it would postpone the project of creating a multicultural residential area by another 20 years.

Segregated residential areas lead to another problem — segregated schools. Many Muslim parents are trying to enrol their children in better schools, but these are outside the Asian residential areas, hence they generally fall foul of the catchment area rules. Even if they are successful, they find that their children encounter difficulties in adapting to suddenly being in an exclusively white environment. Many parents feel that the catchment area rules are there to protect middle-class schools from an invasion of working-class children and, worse still, working-class Asian children. This is helping to maintain both the differences in educational achievement between working-class and middle-class children and racial segregation.

> 'For most Muslims, all avenues for interaction with the white community — whether it is living, learning or working together — are closed'

Twenty-five years ago, our local primary school, St Andrew's, had a 50-50 ratio of white and Asian students. It inculcated a mutual respect between the different cultures and the pupils got to know each other well. In 2003, this school had only 16 white students remaining on its register.

Poor schooling translates into poorly paid jobs, or no jobs at all, which ensures no escape from existing residential areas; hence the vicious circle is complete. Even those who have gained university education complain that if their degree is from anything other than the most established universities, private sector companies are not willing to recruit them and give them that crucial first break they need to establish themselves within a profession. In desperation, some move to London in search of opportunities.

For most Muslims, all avenues for interaction with the white community — whether it is living, learning or working together — are closed. Politicians and policy-makers must take prompt action to reverse these trends. Schools and offices allow intermingling in a disciplined and controlled environment that must precede attempts to create mixed residential areas. Current attempts at bringing people together — for example, annual inter-faith walks and Eid dinners — are a tribute to the good intentions of the organisers, but the attendees are usually the already converted.

The second question is why is the educational achievement of the Muslim community so low? This has become one of the most bitter and difficult debates in Keighley. Transcontinental marriages have repeatedly been singled out as a major cause; our local Labour MP Ann Cryer has made the direct link between marriages with partners from Pakistan and "economic and social underachievement" in the Asian community. The argument is that transcontinental marriages lead to limited use of English in Muslim homes, which permanently and irreversibly hampers children's education. This in turn stunts their ability to achieve within wider society.

Educational underachievement in the Muslim community is undeniable, but if its sole cause were transcontinental marriages, it would be exclusive to Keighley's Muslim-dominated schools. Government statistics show that this is not the case; poor, white, working-class areas of Bradford have comparably low educational achievement.

Analyse the performance at the primary school I mentioned above, St Andrew's, and some interesting issues emerged. The Ofsted report for St Andrew's describes the five-year-olds who enter the school as having "little or no English". Yet in only two years' time, when these children sit Key Stage 1 tests, they are "close to [national] average in reading and above [national] average in writing". In two years, the lingual disadvantage has been wiped out.

The teachers have taken positive measures, including investing resources into an intelligent literacy strategy. Ninety-one per cent of students achieved national curriculum level 2 (the level expected from most seven-year-olds), while the students of Guard House primary, whose exclusively white students are from "an extensive estate of council-owned housing", achieved 71%. It appears that children born to parents involved in a transcontinental marriage are outperforming white children from a similar socio-economic background.

What is surprising is that although seven-year-old Muslims have "caught up" with white students, key stage 2 results from 11-year-olds suggest that Muslim students fall behind in the years from seven to 11. Figures for 2004 show that only 72% of St Andrew's students achieve national curriculum level 4 in English (the level expected from most 11-year-olds). Although this represents a drop from achievement at key stage 1, it is still 19% higher than Guard House.

The fall in achievement from key stage 1 and 2 seems odd given that we would expect lingual handicaps to have the greatest effect in the early years of a child's education. The Ofsted report explains this deviance as follows: "[The] teaching is not quite as thorough and well organised [at key stage 2] as it is in the earlier years... teachers sometimes have to work hard to maintain order and motivate pupils."

The Ofsted team's explanation hints at a serous problem, the decline of motivation and discipline as children get older. Parents commonly claim that as their children grow up, they "lose control". This is the consequence of the environmental forces acting on their children becoming stronger. An environment of educational underachievement, crime, joblessness and lack of role models undermines the educational ambition that the school and parents had nurtured. Educational underachievement becomes acceptable and, in some cases, the norm. Because Muslim and white communities served by St Andrew's and Guard House share almost equally in these factors, their children's education suffers in similar proportions. The point is that having a mother or a father who is not fluent in English is not a huge disadvantage, but having parents who are not sufficiently educated in any country is.

The onus is upon educated Muslims to provide solutions to their community's problems. The Abu Zahra Foundation which I set up with a group of other Keighley-born young professionals is one such attempt. It provides Islamic education to children exclusively in the English language. The Abu Zahra staff teach an understanding of Islam that is both moderate and relevant to the lives of Muslim children in Keighley.

Classes and public lectures are held for adults, men and women, discussing topical issues with the intention of providing a catalyst for fruitful debate within the community. Other activities include trips exploring English heritage, activities in the countryside, providing positive role models, informal career advice and job networks.

The aim is to counter the disadvantages faced by the children in our community and to demonstrate that being a devout Pakistani Muslim, rooted in Keighley, and being English, is achievable.

Who is talking to whom and about what?
Madeleine Bunting

All too often, the conclusion to difficult discussions about the place of Muslims in British society end with a call for more debate. It has become the instant response, a panacea for every kind of challenge to patterns of identity, belonging, integration and interaction. But the question is where does the debate happen? And if the debate doesn't happen, why doesn't it happen? Who talks to whom and about what?

In November 2004, the Guardian and Barrow Cadbury drew together over 100 young Muslims to discuss issues such as their sense of identity and social cohesion. (The report of that event, Young, Muslim and British, is reproduced in the addendum.) The aim was to pull as wide a range of young Muslims together as possible and provide them with a public platform to debate the crucial issues affecting their community. Such was the enthusiastic response to this event that the Guardian has decided to make a Young Muslim Forum an annual event.

For this book, I asked three participants of the Guardian's Young Muslim Forum to reflect on their own experience of debate. In discussions with them, it was clear that they saw the Muslim community involved in two interrelated strands of thought and discussion; first and foremost, an internal debate about its understanding of Islam and how to be a Muslim in secular Britain. Where does this debate take place — within the family? Close friends? The mosque? Both Ehsan Masood and Farah Khan describe in this section how this debate gets circumscribed and struggles to reach honest maturity. One of the common remarks after the Guardian/Barrow Cadbury event in 2004 was the useful role that institutions outside the Muslim community could play in facilitating this internal dialogue.

Second, the three talk of the debate between Muslim and non-Muslim. This is the debate we may see on our television screens or read about in the media; the problem is that it is a debate that casts many crucial potential participants in the role of passive spectators. What seems a pressing priority is to promote and facilitate the debate at a personal, local level, away from the media spotlight. This is the debate that shapes perception and behaviour, and, crucially, has the capacity to change minds. That debate may be incorporated into the day-to-day interactions of neighbours, in shops and on the street. It does not have to require deep conversations on the beliefs of Islam — perceptions can develop from living alongside someone and getting to know them.

But Asim Siddiqui and Farah Khan describe how the kind of conversations — between work colleagues, friends or neighbours — that could build greater understanding don't usually happen spontaneously; not even university manages to foster the kind of interaction one might expect, writes Siddiqui.

So there is an urgent question of just how are people to build greater mutual understanding of each other, Muslim and non-Muslim? What are the processes to achieve this? Who is going to do it and how?

'This is the debate that shapes perception and behaviour, and, crucially, has the capacity to change minds'

Farah Khan

I was born into a culture where the idea of challenging your parents on any matter is considered a heresy, yet I live in a country where the questioning of accepted wisdom is the orthodoxy. In an environment where deference to elders and authority still hold sway, how and where do young Muslims begin to address the conflicts that arise from being both British and Muslim?

For our parents' generation, those questions never arose: their culture, their thinking and their home was always the motherland. They undoubtedly faced racism, but their religion — which governs every aspect of their lives and provides a lens through which to view the world — was never a matter of public concern. Most early Muslim immigrants did not pass through the British education system and were therefore never exposed, in their impressionable years, to the contradictions of a way of life totally alien to their own. Nor did they find themselves torn between those two worlds, forced to choose between doing what was expected of them and what they would like: acceptance from their British peers. But is it possible to be both British and Muslim? Can Muslims integrate without losing their faith? Where do Muslims talk and debate these questions and what are the questions which most preoccupy the Muslims I know?

First, within the family and among close relatives, we never talk about our identity as British Muslims. Identity only becomes an issue, something to be questioned and analysed, when others challenge it. Besides, Islam discourages nationalism, preferring us to consider other Muslims around the world as part of our family, the ummah. The one political discussion that does take place, particularly among male relatives, is the plight of other members of the ummah and international relations.

But what we do discuss in detail is the practical living of our Islamic faith in non-Muslim Britain. Since Islam governs every aspect of our lives, it tends to crop up a great deal in conversation. Parents are always instructing children on how to practise their faith, from how to pray and dress appropriately to eating with your right hand. Despite being a mother of two, I still get calls from my mother asking me how many times I have prayed that day and beseeching me to make more time for reading the Qu'ran!

Grandparents often teach their grandchildren how to recite verses from the Qu'ran and the minutiae of ritual which often get overlooked by parents. Uncles often talk about Islamic history and politics. There are conversations between teenagers and parents over religious restrictions on matters that conflict with British norms of behaviour, such as socialising, relationships with the opposite sex and dress code.

Siblings and friends frequently confer about the difficulties of practising the faith in a secular society. For example, what do they do about praying at work? How do they get out of shaking a man's hand without causing offence? (A common ploy is hold a drink in one hand and a folder

'Despite being a mother of two, I still get calls from my mother asking me how many times I have prayed that day'

or handbag in another.) For those with children, the topics that crop up include: do they allow their children to take part in the Christmas play? What are they going to do about swimming lessons for their adolescent daughters (since they will have to wear swimming costumes)? Will they be sending their children to single or mixed secondary schools?

Underlying these conversations is a lot of fear. It is not that Muslims cannot question – it is that they are scared of where that questioning might lead. This fear has its roots in Islamic teachings about *bidah*, or religious innovation, which the prophet Muhammad warned against, saying, "every newly invented matter is an innovation, and every innovation is misguidance and every misguidance leads to hellfire."

Another saying attributed to the prophet states that at the end of the world, the Muslim community will split into 73 different sects and that only one of them – the main body of the Muslims, al Jama'ah, will enter paradise. Muslims are therefore terrified of reforming Islam in case they end up in one of the 72 sects who enter hell. People are very scared, then, to do the right thing, and seek reassurance from each other.

The public debate within the Muslim community

The debate about British Muslim identity has been growing over the past decade, as Muslim academics and intellectuals have attempted to address the challenges facing believers as they try to accommodate their faith with modernity. The subject has become popular in Muslim newspapers and magazines, while those with access to the internet can also participate in online debates on a plethora of Islamic and non-Islamic websites, including Muslim News online, Open Democracy and Qantara De.

However, two large sections of the community have so far been absent from these debates: the disproportionately high numbers of Muslims who are unemployed, or trapped in low-skilled jobs; and women. Neither are prominent in the public debates within the Muslim community. The mosque could play a crucial role in drawing in these elements of the community to participate in discussion.

But what particularly concerns me is just how limited the debate is within the Muslim community. Here in the north-east of England, there is a growing incidence of violence and intimidation by racists, with Cumbria, Northumbria, Durham and Cleveland topping the table of the 10 most dangerous places for ethnic minorities to live in Britain. The far right BNP is active in Sunderland, targeting Muslims in its hate campaigns by exploiting the lack of a law of incitement to religious hatred.

But instead of addressing these very real problems, the Newcastle Muslim community prefers to concentrate its energies on the correct practice of religious rituals and the permissibility of various consumer products. The amount of time wasted on trivial matters is unbelievable when there are so many urgent matters at hand. Only last week, I received a call from a friend who, having watched the Islam satellite channel, was concerned that the manufacturing process of vinegar may deem it *haram* (forbidden)! Another friend raised the question of perfume. Since it contained alcohol, were we allowed to wear it? I had to restrain myself!

However, it is not all bad news. The Sunderland Bangladeshi centre is a shining example of best practice. Located in an area of high unemployment and low educational achievement, it is also home to over a thousand asylum seekers – fertile ground for conflict. When it became

'The amount
of time
wasted on
trivial
matters is
unbelievable
when there
are so many
urgent
matters
at hand'

the focus of a BNP hate campaign, it created opportunities for joint activities with white communities, organised cultural events and made their facilities available to the entire community. The result is tangible — better interaction between communities, better race relations and therefore less social tension.

Engagement with non-Muslims

At a time when Muslims can be perceived as the enemy within and when Islam is being caricatured in the media as unremittingly dogmatic, oppressive and incompatible with democracy and the "basic values of Britishness", the urgency for constructive engagement with non-Muslims becomes ever greater.

Increasingly, I value the contribution that culture and the arts can make to breaking down barriers. This year I was deeply moved to see a mainly white audience at the BBC3 World Music awards at the Sage, Gateshead, rise up and dance to the Arab pop songs of Algerian rai superstar Khaled. The fact that he was a Muslim did not matter — his music spoke their language and they demanded an encore.

The black community has managed to gain greater acceptance through its involvement in sport and music. Black sports stars and musicians now have a diverse fan base and most of British society values their achievements. Even more notable is the Jewish community's contribution to British culture. The image of boxer Amir Khan wrapped in a union flag in the Olympic ring, being cheered on by largely white middle-class males, illustrates that there is no contradiction in being both British and Muslim. We need more public figures to break down barriers and make the wider community aware that our shared values far outweigh our differences.

British Muslims find it difficult to see the opportunities opened up by music, art and literature; many question the permissibility of them. They lay claim to what was once theirs — the great scientific, cultural and artistic achievements of the Islamic world, which during the dark ages, provided the spark for the western renaissance. They should recognise that culture — in all its forms — crosses language and faith barriers and as such, should be used to bring communities together to build trust, create alliances and facilitate opportunities for debate. As Thomas Mann said: "Speech is civilisation itself. The word, even the most contradictory word, preserves contact — it is silence which isolates."

Ehsan Masood

Muslim scholars often like to proclaim, not without a hint of pride, that Islam has no priesthood. This means that in theory, we are free to choose how we practise the faith; how we interpret the Qur'an; and the lessons we can draw from the life of Muhammad, the prophet. Islam doesn't have the equivalent of a Pope, a central authority figure that the faithful can turn to for advice, guidance, blessings and to set some basic rules. I like to think that this allows ordinary people of all ages and walks of life to have greater control of their lives. It means we can interpret the faith whichever way we see fit, according to our own conscience, experience and understanding.

But in practice, we are surrounded by a network of gates and gate-keepers, including family elders, mosque imams and sheikhs that stand in the way of individual Muslims who want to ask questions of the faith, take it in new directions and engage more closely with modernity.

Followers of Shia and Ismaili Islam have evolved parallel systems of clerical hierarchy. And the hundreds of millions of followers of the Sufi branches of Sunni Islam, too, often defer important personal decisions to third parties that many regard as living (or deceased) saints. Many non-Sufi Sunnis (such as the revivalist Tablighis) are similarly reluctant to stray too far from the doctrine handed down from their founding fathers.

And herein lies part of the "problem" that British (and non-British) Muslims face today. There is a debate on issues of faith that needs to happen, but has yet to begin among British Muslims. As a community we are still young, feel vulnerable and not yet secure enough in our new settings. We are too busy holding government and other authorities to account and feel no need to ask difficult questions of each other. These questions include: who has authority to define whether someone can call themselves a Muslim? What is sharia and can it be applied in today's world? And who has the right to define what can and cannot be labelled Islamic? The few who are calling for such a debate to happen believe that it needs to be an internal one for Muslims alone, away from the gaze of mainstream Britain.

Yet this debate has started in the wider Muslim world and it is a very public one in Egypt, Iran and Lebanon. It is happening now, in part, because of public dissatisfaction with authoritarian regimes in these countries. After decades of repression, people in these countries want social and political change; and the Muslims among them want this change to happen under the guiding influence of Islam. A catalyst for change is undoubtedly the Bush administration's long shadow in the Arabic-speaking world, cast in the wake of the 9/11 attacks.

Where does that leave British Muslims? Could such a debate begin here? Is there a need? Should the debate remain an "internal" one, as some would prefer; or should it take place in full public view? And what should be the role of external organisations?

My own view is that such a debate is unlikely to happen without a

> '**We are too busy holding government and other authorities to account and feel no need to ask difficult questions of each other**'

degree of (admittedly careful) external prodding; and that such a debate must happen in public. The external influence is already there, thanks to the efforts of institutions such as the Guardian, the many government agencies that now work closely with Muslims, as well as the British Council, which tries to represent Muslim Britain in its overseas work.

These institutions may not know it, but their deepening interaction with British Muslims is leading to much reflection and soul-searching within Britain's different Muslim community organisations and a realisation that we have much to learn. Many of our community leaders, even a decade ago, were set on a path of isolation. They felt that the solutions to our many (particularly economic and social problems) were fully contained in the pages of Islam and included keeping a healthy distance from mainstream Britain. Interaction with indigenous British institutions has helped to change this view.

The debate, moreover, must happen in public (as it is, for example on Channel 4's excellent late-night Shariah TV show), because to keep it internal would also mean keeping it exclusive to a small group. There is, moreover, no such thing as private in today's wired world. Those who want to keep it in the family are often the same people who have most to lose by participation from a wider public.

Above all, the debate needs to happen because far too many Muslims (in Britain and elsewhere) want to reclaim ownership of a faith that gives them the right to choose their own futures. Reclaiming that right means taking back Islam from the many popes and supreme governors that we have allowed to take root in our seminaries, mosques and homes.

Asim Siddiqui

I grew up in the 1980s and remember attending the Muslim Institute's world seminars in London with my family not long after I was out of my nappies. The speeches there described a battle of global proportions, an epic struggle between Islam and the west, the oppressed Muslims versus the oppressors, good versus evil and only we had God on our side. My father (Dr Ghayasuddin Siddiqui) was active in the Islamic movement and known by many of its leaders across the Muslim world. He was passionate about his work and many a dinner table discussion revolved around the plight of the Muslim condition, the intellectual decline and how Muslims could find their feet again to begin the slow trek to recovery. Some of his passion rubbed off on me.

The Islamic revolution in Iran had swept Imam Khomeini to power and had given political Islam its first success story after centuries of defeat. The talk was how Iran-style revolutions would sweep across the Muslim world creating Islamic states that would bring down western civilisation and create a pure Islamic order in its place. Conflict not consensus was the name of the game. It felt so exciting. It was easy to divide the world with black-and-white answers. It was too early for anyone to notice that this talk would seed the intellectual roots that would radicalise a new generation of British Muslims for whom the west would become both their home and their enemy.

I went to University College London and what struck me, having attended an almost all-white grammar school, was how cosmopolitan it was — a real reflection of the wider ethnic make-up of the country. However, I also noticed that many of the various ethnic and religious groups appeared to be more comfortable among their own groups. This could be observed by where people sat at lectures and whom they socialised with in the evenings. The political or religious would busy themselves in their own religious societies surrounded by like-minded people. The only forms of engagement I can remember were the "debates" organised by the Islamic society with non-Muslim speakers. These were invariably deigned to show the "superiority" of Muslims and our "way of life", rather than any genuine attempt at bringing people together and respecting differences. The only time we would want to meet them was to convert them. The lack of non-Muslim contacts would become apparent when the numerous *da'wah* (inviting non-Muslims to Islam) events were almost exclusively attended by Muslims.

The war in Bosnia was raging when I was at university. The genocide of Bosnian Muslims by Serbs (with help from the Croats) with the west sitting idly by enraged us. "If they weren't Muslims, the west would have intervened ages ago," was a common complaint underlying the commonly held view that Islam was the west's new enemy. This somehow reaffirmed the validity of our faith: because only we had truth on our side, we must be the chosen enemies of the west. The other conflicts in the world that did not involve Muslims did not appear on our radar screens.

'During university, the only time we would want to meet non-Muslims was to convert them'

The problem was that as soon as a political opinion was wrapped up and presented in religious terms, who could disagree? I remember coming out of Friday prayers and being handed two leaflets by different groups on the same issue and each coming to different conclusions. Both cited "evidences" from the same Qur'an and Hadith to back up their cases. It was from then on that I became more sceptical and I decided that an argument had to be logical and coherent for it to carry any weight in my eyes; simply reciting verses from the Qur'an was not good enough any more.

Once in a job, I found that discussions about my faith were rare. Partly it was because there wasn't much spare time with the pressures of a job. Partly it was because the social side of most jobs is in the pub and this is where Muslims have a lot of difficulties. Muslims don't particularly want to go to the pub on Friday night — there is only so much pleasure to be had from endless glasses of orange juice. This has a knock-on effect on their progress in the workplace. It also cuts out possibilities for conversations on how non-Muslims view Islam and Muslims. It takes courage on both sides to have frank and open discussion on these issues as it could, if misunderstood, affect how colleagues work together.

One of the reasons that I and a group of other professionals founded the City Circle in 1999 was to offer Muslims in central London a "halal alternative" to the Friday night pub culture. A place where Muslims could hang out and relax without the fear of being led astray. There were religious talks designed to drum in the message of our "Muslimness". There were some initial issues as to where women should be seated — at the back or separately alongside the men. However, it was not long before these were overcome as Muslim women were quick to head up community projects and set the agenda.

The aim was to provide a vehicle for Muslims to fully engage with mainstream societies and civic institutions and to develop a greater knowledge of social and welfare issues affecting all of the community — Muslim and non-Muslim. For example, we were one of the first Muslim groups to engage with environmental issues by putting on a debate in 2000 with George Monbiot. After 9/11, an anti-war group was developed — which went on to join the Stop the War coalition. It triggered debate about the idea of working so closely with non-Muslims — and much confusion. (To deal with this, the City Circle organised a conference in November 2001 on "Islam and the peace movement — where do we stand?", inviting Muslim scholars to justify the positions we were taking.) The process towards greater engagement was never going to be easy and had to be fought every step of the way if we wanted to take our constituents with us. Our religious speakers were called upon to explain — with evidence from the Qur'an and Hadith — that the steps we were taking were right and necessary.

The City Circle encourages Muslims to be more open-minded, self-critical and less holier-than-thou. Speakers are urged to be bold and radical in their talks, and the City Circle has emerged as a laboratory of ideas experimenting how far Muslims feel they can go. For example, one talk in 2004 by a leading Salafi scholar was on "the Muslim obsession with themselves". Such criticism of "religious" Muslims would previously have been considered treason. More traditional talks reassure audiences of our Islamic roots.

The City Circle's approach is to offer a platform to highlight and debate wider concerns — not to impose solutions, but to ask the right questions.

'It takes courage on both sides to have a frank and open discussion on these issues'

How can Muslims best add value to British society? Does citizenship entail any restriction and responsibilities upon British Muslims? How can one be both British and Muslim and contribute fully to both "worlds"? How can Islam's PR in the world be improved? Is it all media bias or have Muslim contributed to this malaise?

The history of the City Circle to date is a microcosm of what is taking place within the wider Muslim community. A number of grassroots groups inspired by the City Circle are emerging up and down the country acting as bridgeheads between their local communities and the wider non-Muslim population.

Habits of solidarity
Ash Amin

Islamophobia, like so many of our other current folk devils – be they asylum, immigration, rioting youths, or the homeless – draws on a misanthropy that has become pervasive in the west. We have come to only like our few friends and family, to associate with those like us and to identify with imagined communities that are an extension of some aspects of ourselves (professionally, ethnically, behaviourally, bodily, etc). From time to time we are moved by the plight of distant others, but on the whole, and for most of the time, we love to hate. We don't like our neighbours, we studiously avoid eye contact in public places, we rant and rail at all manner of types on television, we loathe others on the road, we get irritated in restaurants, we are quick to pass judgment on just about everything that moves, we are suspicious of those in authority, and so on. In brief, we hate difference in a world increasingly viewed down the wrong end of the telescope. There is no single or simple reason behind this rampant misanthropy, but there are many suspects. These include the effects of unrestrained individualism and the cult of self, the demise of universal values of social integration and cohesion – secular or Christian – and the rise of consumer identities which have displaced a love of people for a love of things. It is also the child of a politics of choice which has eroded a sense of the shared or common purpose, and broken down the idea of society as an indivisible whole, and ingrained a view of society as something that those like me are owed (rather than our obligations to others). It thrives on a public culture that endorses tribal behaviour, prejudice in public, pious opinion, and egotistic fantasy amid a new cult of personality which has displaced the cult of ideas and social movements. The list could go on.

The misanthropy, however, comes with a distinctive hierarchy with some despised more than others. Historically, the figure of the stranger, conjured up as a boundary object to demarcate a definable and safe inside from a wild and unknown outside, has been the most feared and hated. The current populist rant against immigrants, asylum seekers, and Gypsies digs deep into this social pathology, underpinned by visceral anxieties of threat, loss or insecurity triggered by the figure of the stranger. Everyday negotiations of difference in public spaces and in public culture and the unstoppable mixing of cultural practices brought about by globalisation, constantly jostle against this hum of anxiety, resulting in a mood of resigned tolerance or hostility shaped by the stance taken by those in a position to influence public opinion. But on matters of race and ethnicity, the balance is always tottered on a very fine point, for in Britain the immigrant stranger has had to contend with an enduring legacy of White Nation, forged during and after empires; whiteness as the prime marker of national belonging and citizenship.

Paul Gilroy has described this condition as a form of post-colonial melancholia, a subliminal yearning for a time of national unity and greatness in denial of Britain's mixed ethnic and cultural heritage. The

> 'Historically, the figure of the stranger has been the most feared and hated'

melancholia plays on the certitudes of Albion: empire read as a just British irradiation; and the subjugated as infantile, barbaric, possibly exotic, but always irreconcilably different. It projects a romanticised time of white national comfort and unity gathered around such icons as green and pleasant land, monarchy and regal pomp, war-time unity and a popular culture of homely restraint, working-class humour, and cheeky urchins. The result has been the displacement of transcultural norms of attachment — secular or otherwise — in defining Britishness, by a set of narrowly defined heritage markers. As a consequence, the assumption is that things will never be the same again, or that non-whites in Britain can never fully belong or must become white in the above senses to qualify as one of us. This is what allows so many in this country to remain anxious beyond proportion about the presence of visible minorities and to turn a blind eye to benign as well as institutionalised racism.

But there is more. What has made the culture of white anxiety decidedly frightening in recent times is its linkage with a new white Christian-cum-military ethos of superiority borne out of the so-called war on terror. Suspicion of difference now finds legitimacy in the comfort zone of the argument that western civilisation is incompatible with, and under threat from, the Orient, now reconfigured as hostile Islam, anti-western Muslims, Asian flu epidemics and unknown germs, and failed autocracies of various kinds. This is one of the principal achievements of the Bush-Blair response to Afghanistan, Iraq, the Palestine-Israel conflict, and 9/11. It has unleashed a new US-driven imperial geopolitics that has little tolerance for soft diplomacy based on multilateralism, internationalism and respect for cultural difference. In Britain too, despite the scale of opposition to the war in Iraq, government propaganda on the terrorist threat, linked in timely fashion to the demand for proof and loyalty from asylum seekers and immigrants and to hysteria in the populist media against multi-ethnic mixture, has managed to produce a new mood of righteous indignation defending Albion in the face of threat. In the name of a safe and stable community, a new security state has emerged unperturbed about rolling back civil liberties and rights, suspicious of Islam, Muslims, foreigners, unruly behaviour, and cosmopolitanism, all rolled together.

The combined effect of the pathology of hate, post-colonial melancholia and new imperial superiority, is that the daily reality of multiculturalism within our borders and of cosmopolitan linkage beyond our borders, has become an object of anxiety. This is dangerous and must be opposed, for the cornerstone of a secure and forward-looking Britain has to be a plural and open polity that is confident with the clash of difference. We must be willing to celebrate a deracialised idea of national belonging (an ethos of cosmopolitan solidarity, and experiments of grounded interculturalism). How can this ethos be advanced and by whom? First, blind declarations of old universals such as secularism, omniscience or transcendence will not do, partly because multiculturalism has exposed their limits, and also because even the most high-minded daily fall short of practising these ideals. Instead, steady work is required to convert misanthropy and anxiety into an ethos of getting along and together. A basic requirement — as ever — is to ensure that all are given the means of flight and security, that is, the chance to aspire and become something else without fear and anxiety. The link between individual security and social wellbeing is incontrovertible. In terms of what should be done, the usual suspects come to mind, ranging from ensuring that

> **'Without a discussion of the familiar and the strange, the danger of slipping back into culturally, ethnically and racially coded definitions of national belonging will remain high'**

those who face disadvantage are provided with access to good education, housing, public and welfare services and job opportunities, to guaranteeing a framework for social justice that comprehensively cracks down on all forms of prejudice and discrimination, popular and institutional. But, considerable work is also needed to publicise that the support provided is not only for minorities, but also for poor whites stuck in similar circuits of deprivation and exclusion, so that the sting can be taken out of the politics of envy and hate that thrives on want.

Second, all manner of small local inventions are needed to engender the habit of living with difference through promotion of some form of connection between strangers, so that strangeness ceases to be an object of fear. Multicultural and multi-ethnic Britain daily negotiates difference in its public spaces, schools, workplaces, and varied virtual sites. These are by no means spaces of happy collective dancing around the multicultural maypole, but they do reveal a grounded habit of getting along and getting by. This sociality is more pervasive than the cultural isolationism and social segregation that exists in particular parts of Britain and among particular communities. Actions designed for the latter, be they gated, middle-class communities, white flight retreats, or segregated poor inner-city neighbourhoods, can build on the dynamics of prosaic negotiations of difference in everyday life.

They can do so first by bringing people from different backgrounds to work together in projects of common interest in ordinary spaces of habitual encounter. Typical examples include experimenting with mixed sports teams in schools and colleges, cultural exchanges in creches, food from around the world in communal gardens, fusion music in youth clubs, multicultural events in housing estates. In turn, experiments can be designed to engineer displacement from the daily rut, to spark cultural transgression among those most locked into a spiral of hate and suspicion. Here, too, there are many examples from around the world that can be drawn upon, including imaginative uses of sporting events and public art to bring together warring youth factions, world-music concerts in hospitals to break down barriers when the guard is down, urban visuals to display or iconicise mixity and hybridity where most needed, or schemes for the recalcitrant that demand civic duty for a sustained period. Current public policy based on spatial solutions — for example, via mixed housing estates and multicultural public spaces — falls short of the interculturalism that draws on shared participation.

Third, the language of national belonging has to jettison its white nostalgic overtones, if the grounded experience of living with diversity in so many cities and communities in Britain is to be given a chance. There is much that the government and other opinion formers can do to rebut the idea that the nation has fallen from a state of perfection (cultural or political), replacing it with the idea that we are a people to come, defined through the varied practices and geographies of attachment of the diverse people who find themselves in Britain. In a world riddled with mixity and movement, there is everything to be gained in defining the nation as a nexus of many spatial connections (local, national, European, transatlantic, transnational) and many nationalities and cultural practices (which obviates the need to define a cultural heartland), and as an emblem of unity stripped of myths of origin or ethnic/racial hierarchy. For a country such as ours, steeped as it is in colonial melancholia, this is an imperative, requiring new ideas of solidarity and obligation that come without the baggage of particularist national traditions. The celebrated Scottish Enlightenment economist Adam Smith's insistence on sympathy as the necessary glue in a market economy is one place to start, but there are also other metaphors circulating in current academic debate that place the ethics of inter-subjectivity at the centre of definitions of (national) belonging. This might involve publicity for the idea that subjectivity itself, in needing the other to be called forth, necessitates an ethic of unconditional hospitality towards the stranger. These are abstract principles that need considerable working through (for example, in policies and actions that openly stand for mutuality, shared rights, and engagement as equals between all of Britain's cultural and ethnic communities). However, what is clear is that without a discussion of the familiar and the strange at this level, the danger of slipping back into culturally/ethnically/racially coded definitions of national belonging will remain high.

Finally, a new public ethos that bridges difference will help to pave the way for a definition of citizenship in a multi-ethnic and multicultural society based on shared political understandings of the good life. A consensus on what it means to be British is required not on grounds of race, colour, creed, religion, or cultural heritage, but on core principles of political culture relating to individual and collective freedom, citizenship and residence, rules of private and public engagement, incitement, prejudice and violence, standards of public provision, and so on. The irony is that many of these elements are already in place, but has come to be overshadowed by an ethno-cultural obsession with what counts as Britishness. They could be gathered into a new constitutional settlement that is periodically amended and reviewed as British social life evolves in new directions.

Conclusion

No doubt the debate on the future of multi-ethnic societies will continue to be framed around the respective strengths of multiculturalist, assimilationist and universalist modes of social integration. But in some ways, all three have also been superseded by the times: assimilationism by the trend of irreversible post-national/transnational affiliation and the rise of nation as a "community of communities", as Lord Parekh has noted; universalism by a genuine excess of unassimilated difference, a suspicion of universals that are meant to capture the interests of all but rarely do so (for example, the Eurocentrism of enlightenment ideas), and a felt clash between secular and religious ideals; and multiculturalism by majoritarian melancholia anxiety as well as minoritarian suspicion of its paternalistic concessions. Most importantly, a new political economy of hate sparked by 9/11 and other related events has emerged, gathered around the fault line of religious, civilisational, and ethno-nationalist division. These new circumstances call for a new approach to living with difference, based on habits of solidarity that negotiate ethnic and cultural difference and the normality of the stranger. No doubt this is a utopian ideal placed in the way of the powerful new security state that is bent on crusader puritanism but is one rooted in a grounded conviviality that could become a national habit given the chance.

Addendum
The Guardian forum, November 2004, "Young, Muslim and British"

Young, Muslim and British

Madeleine Bunting

Published
30/11/04
The Guardian

The "war on terror" has put British Muslims under the spotlight as never before. But the post 9/11 debates among Muslims on faith, identity and integration are rarely heard in the mainstream media. We invited 100 young Muslims to discuss the main issues shaping their lives — and their futures

The idea was a bold gamble, but within minutes the calm murmur of eight simultaneous conversations on different themes in a hall in London last week indicated that it was, in some way, paying off: young British Muslims were talking and we were listening.

We weren't sure of the questions, we certainly didn't expect easy answers, but we had two objectives. We wanted to catch a glimpse — to eavesdrop — on how a set of issues are being debated within a new generation of British Muslims, and then, through our reporting, we wanted a non-Muslim readership to hear voices rarely heard. So the Guardian played honest broker, inviting as wide a range of young Muslims with a potential to shape their community's future as we could reach.

The 103 British Muslims who joined us last week could be described as among the success stories of two decades of integration: from mostly humble backgrounds, they have got to university, or are working in jobs as diverse as accountants, pharmacists, social workers, journalists, civil servants, lawyers, nurses and entrepreneurs. Alongside their academic and career achievements they have drawn from their faith a powerful social conscience; the majority of our participants devote a considerable amount of their time to volunteering in community organisations and political campaigns.

This is a pivotal generation; they have the skills and education that many of their parents lacked to make their experience heard. And that experience will increasingly be one which will have international resonance: the two civilisations of Islam and the west are not abstract concepts to them, but the influences they daily negotiate in their own lives. How they vote, how they dress, how they pray, who they befriend and who they marry: all are influenced by the accommodation they find between the two, at a time when, internationally, the two are being set in violent opposition.

They open a new chapter in Britain's complex history of race and multiculturalism: how we negotiate a faith-based political identity. On this, there are no inspirations we can borrow from abroad as we did a generation ago with the US's civil rights movement. This phase of how to accommodate diversity and equality within a western democracy is a chapter which has to be written in Europe, as one of the five invited panellists, the Swiss-born philosopher Tariq Ramadan, made clear in the final plenary of our debate.

As the conversations got under way, two features of this gathering were immediately striking. The first was its diversity: the astonishing range of background, from west Africa to the Middle East, Pakistan and

> 'The two civilisations of Islam and the west are not abstract concepts to them, but the influences they daily negotiate'

Bangladesh, from Morocco to Turkish Cyprus, and English converts. Just as striking — though its significance much harder to read — was the variety in how women dressed, from the carefully pinned hijab to the long hair and the braided extensions, from long skirts to jeans.

The second feature was the appetite for debate. It needed no prompting, rather the reverse: the difficulty was in ensuring that everyone had their say. The unmistakable impression is that this is a generation that relishes the heavy responsibility they bear. Some perceive the international resonances of what they are developing — others do not. What they are all acutely aware of is its implications within Britain; it is the quest for justice for a marginalised, misrepresented, impoverished, and increasingly beleaguered community that spurs them on.

Our participants are well aware that they are the products of a polarised generation. For every person in the room that evening, there are thousands of other young Muslims who are trapped in low-skilled jobs or are unemployed. We now know (the statistics have only begun to reflect a breakdown according to faith) that 36% of British Muslims are leaving school with no qualifications, while one-fifth of 16- to 24-year-old Muslims in Britain are unemployed. Forty per cent of British Muslims are in low-skilled jobs and nearly 70% of Bangladeshi and Pakistani children live in poverty. A British Muslim generation is coming of age — one-third of the community is under 15 — with the experience of deprivation.

That poverty haunted the debate, and what cropped up on many of the tables was a sense of frustration at what participants perceive as the failures of their own community. Sometimes harshly self-critical, they talked of low educational expectations, a lack of ambition and, most importantly, a failure to pull together to improve their lot; unfavourable comparisons were drawn with Jewish and Indian minorities.

Insecure, lacking self-confidence, haunted by failure and by personal experiences of deprivation, racism and, since 9/11, oppressive anti-terrorist measures and increasing Islamophobia: these are some of the elements that give such compelling force to the common identity this generation finds in being Muslim and the increasing confidence with which they assert it as a political identity.

While "we are Muslims" may offer a place of belonging in an inhospitable country, it is a place riven with conflict. Because defining what it is to be a Muslim is a near impossible task, reverberating around the entire Muslim world; the question of what is the true faith is convulsing the faithful everywhere.

The participants wrestled with the definition of the "keystone issues" on which to unite: Palestine, Iraq and "Muslim values" came one reply. Of all the debates, the one attempting to define Muslim values — whether there could be a "British Islam" — was the most circular, repeatedly snagging on the issue of whether Islam can adapt, or is unchanging in all times and places. The intensity of the struggle within Islam internationally bears heavily on this generation in Britain.

As if all of this were not already complicated enough, this generation is being called to explain their faith to a secular society which has long since lost all interest in God, angels, prophets and holy books. What does it mean to "put God first in everything", as one participant described British Muslims' distinctive contribution to British society? Frequently, issues that the vast majority of Muslims have little interest in debating, such as homosexuality and abortion (such is the consensus, there is nothing to debate) or the role of women (why do they keep ask-

'This generation is being called to explain their faith to a secular society that has long since lost all interest in God'

ing us about this?, they complain) are settled by faith — which only deepens incomprehension among non-Muslims. From there, it's a short step to outright hostility. You could put a devout Muslim and a devout Christian together and, while they might not agree, they could understand much of what the other had to say, but to the broad swath of the secular British, the gulf of incomprehension is gaping — and the onus is all upon the faithful to explain themselves.

This pivotal generation is already defying many of the experts. They are not conforming to the theories of secularisation common for 20 years; they are perhaps even more devout than their parents, and are certainly more assertive of their faith and its requirements. According to our poll, half of British Muslims pray five times a day every day, while 80% pray at least once a day; even allowing for some religious guilt inflating the figures, the evidence is of a level of religious practice that is higher than any other community in the UK. The poll showed that they want public accommodation of their faith — time to pray where they work and sharia courts in Britain for civil cases (as long as the penalties do not contravene criminal law). They are not showing much sign of conforming to earlier patterns of migration and cultural assimilation, while the "war on terror" is radicalising them into a wide range of political activity — from human rights campaigning to radical jihadism.

Who knows how this chapter will take shape? As one participant said, we have the title — British Muslims — but beyond, there are only blank pages.

Madeleine Bunting was awarded the Race in the Media Award June 2005 for the Young, Muslim and British project

The big debate

Eight tables, eight subjects, 103 young Muslims. Here are the reports of the discussions (moderated by participants) and eight personal stories

Raihan Al Faradhi, 19

Student

I am a British Muslim, but only because the sentence "British Muslim" is grammatically more correct than "Muslim British". I live in east London.

When I graduate I want to earn lots of money, but also contribute to the community. It's important there is a purpose to my life and I am working to ensure economic problems are addressed.

My parents came over from Bangladesh in the early 80s to work. My father is a headteacher, and my mother is a classroom assistant. I have four sisters.

Being a Muslim is the overriding factor in the way I live my life. It enables me to contribute positively to society. People perceive it to be a restrictive religion, but it encourages me to try to make a difference in all the spheres of life. It just gives you a sense of being alive.

I went to a private school, and the majority of my friends there were non-Muslims, and this diverse mix has made me who I am today.

I work for several Muslim organisations. One is the Young Muslim Organisation UK, which runs projects on drugs and women. I am also the London representative for the Federation of Student Islamic Societies, as well as being involved in the Islamic student organisation at the London School of Economics.

Photographs: David Levene

Rukshana Ali, 22

Paediatric nurse

Last night a drunk man on the bus accused me of thinking I was Saddam Hussein. He was so drunk he didn't know what he was saying. That's frustrating: the misconceptions people have about my religion.

When I was much younger I didn't even know about Islam. I had this image that it was boring and only for our grandparents' generation. I didn't realise that there was so much emphasis on young people. The youth are really considered important to the community. We shape the future.

I properly got involved in my religion when I was about 14. Being involved in the mosque, and getting a better understanding of my faith, opened me up. It gave me confidence in my faith and identity.

I know where I'm going. I know what the purpose of my existence is. I've found strength from the other young women I have met.

I chair Muslimaat UK, a Muslim women's group which brings together young women for community projects. We work with other young women, who may be struggling with all the normal things that teenagers find hard: friends, bullying, schoolwork, drugs. That's about education and community.

There's this view that there's an older man sitting somewhere making all the decisions, but in a truly Islamic society the youth would be listened to, they would be at the forefront of what's happening. People don't understand that about Islam.

I don't know where all the misconceptions come from. They need clearing up.

Sajjad Hoque, 34
Entrepreneur

I'm pessimistic about the future for Muslims in Britain, so much so that I'm looking to move my business and family to Dubai. We may keep a summer home here but I think our future lies elsewhere.

I was born in Leeds and graduated from University College London. I worked for a number of companies, including the Channel Tunnel, before setting up my own property business. I have a coffee bar in Ealing which serves halal food but is very popular with non-Muslims.

Dubai makes sense from a business point of view — I don't think this government has done much for small businesses. But it goes deeper than that. There, I will be able to practise my religion freely. Before I worked for myself it was not always easy to get time off to go to Friday prayers and so on. Security is also an issue. I think I would feel safer in Dubai.

But what most disturbs me is how Muslim people are being treated by the authorities. I know people who have been subject to security checks as they come into Britain just because they've got a beard. Freedom and equality have made Britain and America great. I fear those qualities are being lost.

I think it's a problem that the Muslim community is not working together effectively. You go to the Regent's Park mosque and see the division in the community.

Ayfer Orhan, 45

Prospective parliamentary candidate

When I first came to the UK aged five, people thought I was mixed race because of my curly hair and olive skin. In those days they didn't know Cyprus existed.

If I was to say I had a Muslim background, most people would be surprised. Maybe there is still a stereotypical concept of what a typical Muslim looks like and I don't fit that.

I help at surgeries held by Joan Ryan, the MP for Enfield North. There is a growing tide of people who look Muslim who are coming to me with concerns about their treatment by frontline council staff. Their perception is they are being discriminated against because of the way they look.

Being born a Muslim has made me far more aware and understanding of different cultures and values.

I am the first Turkish prospective parliamentary candidate in this country, standing for Labour in north-west Cambridgeshire. I hope to be a great role model for other Turkish people.

Turkish Kurds and Cypriots are extremely diverse in their sense of Islam. Some are very devout, but others are non-believers. Because there has always been dialogue, Turkish people are far more ready for a debate than some Muslim cultures, and that's what makes our community very different.

Anber Raz, 28
Policy officer

When I was growing up, Liverpool had very few Asian people. I experienced a lot of racism. Where I lived in Anfield there was a lot of poverty and you had to have bars on your windows and doors. As a child, I was terrified. It tends to make you reserved, unconfident. You don't go out and play.

Coming from an Asian background I found a lot of women were held back from doing things because they were female. I was always told to aspire to achieve your goals, but I found a lot of women were not encouraged like that.

I know people in the Asian community who have suffered from domestic violence and haven't been able to get out.

I studied law at the University of Liverpool and took a master's degree in criminal justice. I left Liverpool in 2002 to work for the UN. I'm now parliamentary affairs policy officer for the Fawcett Society, which does policy work geared towards women's rights. I'd like to do more policy work within the Asian community around domestic violence. We have to say, quite clearly, this is not acceptable.

I'd class myself as Muslim first, then British Asian. The problem I have is that Islam is a humanitarian religion, yet I think we've lost that. As Muslims, we've lost what Islam is about. The way Islam is linked with terrorism is partly a failure of the community.

Ajmal Masroor, 33

Cultural relations consultant, imam

In my college days at Hammersmith, where I studied politics and Arabic, I founded an Islamic society. Before that there was nothing at the college for the Muslim community. Everything changed on 9/11. Extremists among Muslims were giving interviews so I went to the media and insisted they put on mainstream Muslims; I ended up doing the interviews myself.

I came to Britain from Bangladesh when I was one. At nine I went back because my father was afraid we would lose our identity as Muslims. But we returned when I was 13. I experienced racism in the East End of London. There were only two non-white families in the area. I remember bricks being thrown at our doors and our car windows being broken.

I could have become an angry and destructive person. I am lucky I have been able to change the negative experience to go forward fighting those prejudices.

My wife is Hungarian and she has accepted Islam. Our children will inherit a true fusion of culture: Hungarian, Bangladeshi, British, Muslim.

I lead Friday prayers in four mosques across London in rotation. I am called an unconventional imam because I don't get paid, and my sermons are in English.

My aim now is to go into politics. I am a prospective parliamentary candidate for the Lib Dems. Obviously I am disillusioned with Labour.

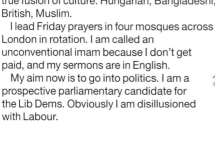

Salma Yaqoob, 33

Psychotherapist

My parents came from Pakistan in the 60s. My dad first worked in a mill and then as a postal worker until he retired. I consider myself to be a British Muslim but I don't like to be pushed into defining myself; it has a dislocating effect. To some, as a Muslim I am either a fanatical terrorist or a victim of Islam, and I am neither of those: we are just people.

I became politically active within two weeks of the 9/11 attacks. I was in Birmingham city centre when this man came up and spat on me. To me, Birmingham was a great place, and I had never experienced any racism or given it a second thought. I began to wonder, where was this all going to lead?

We are living in challenging times. For Muslims it's important to hold a firm and dignified line, between not being reactive to what's happening, but I do think there's injustice. There is a disproportionate response from the government and political ambitions are being put before what is good for humanity.

As Muslims, we have to be confident and not be defensive, we have to be open and not be afraid to say what we feel.

Non-Muslims have also to look at why they are living in a climate of fear. I feel my eyes have been opened. I was very passive before. Now I am vice-chair of Respect, the anti-war alliance. In one sense, ignorance is bliss but I couldn't go back to the way I was before 9/11. I would rather live in a better world than the one we do today.

Asim Siddiqui, 28

Accountant

I grew up in a family that was always concerned about what was going on in the community around them. My father is Dr Ghayasuddin Siddiqui, one of the founders of the Muslim Parliament, and my mother is a social worker. The Muslim Parliament was very provocative when it was first set up.

I'm chair of City Circle, a group of London-based professionals which is involved in social projects. I learnt from my parents a sense of justice and fairness. If God has gifted you in certain ways, you have a responsibility.

I would describe myself as a British Muslim. I don't see any contradiction about the two. I don't agree with Tony Blair about the war in Iraq but neither does Charles Kennedy. I will be a father in February and the thing that concerns me most is schooling. From a list of 10 issues, one might be foreign policy.

I went to school in Buckinghamshire and, unlike my Pakistani friends, I had white friends. I remember instances of racism. One guy told me that he would prefer it if there were no Pakistanis in the UK, except for me and my family! I thought that if we could find the time to speak to English people, even racists, we would melt their hearts at some point. Britain is a nation of immigrants and always will be.

We have to engage. As Churchill said, "jaw-jaw is better than war-war". The bottom line is that we are British.

Table 1: How would you describe your identity?

'I am
absolutely
British. I am
absolutely
Pakistani.
I am
absolutely
Muslim. I am
all of those'

"It is not about what people feel but what they are allowed to feel," said Alya Shakir, a translator, who believes a public declaration of being a "British Muslim" is impossible because of stereotypes surrounding Britishness.

"We are restricted by how people perceive us and what they allow us to be. You can say to people you are British and they will push you for another explanation because we do not fit their idea of what 'British' is."

Such signifiers as an Islamic name or a non-western-looking face provide a ready-made barrier to one's citizenry entitlement, according to Iman Naji, a student at Surrey University. "I was born and brought up here. All I know is a British life, but we have to accept the fact we will never be 100% British."

Raihana Nasreen, a medical student at King's College London, said: "I am Muslim first because I measure everything against that."

Being a British Muslim is an easier space to inhabit in multicultural hotspots such as London and Manchester than the backstreets of Bradford, participants agreed. But what is clear for these second- and third-generation Muslims is that the question of passing the "cricket test", as coined by the former Tory minister Norman Tebbit, has had its day.

Being British can no longer be determined by which team you support in an international game. "That's the politics of empire, the legacy of partition," said Navid Ahkter, a television producer. "It's a very outdated notion to feel we have to go through these tests at all. There are many ways of being British."

Multiple identities for those whose family roots reach abroad can be "comfortably" negotiated, Mr Ahkter added, explaining: "I am absolutely British. I am absolutely Pakistani. I am absolutely Muslim. I am all of those."

"'British Muslim' is a title with an empty page. We have a good opportunity to start defining it," he concluded.

Consensus was more easily reached on a question of whether Muslims should participate in British political life. Speakers revealed frustration at the way the country's 1.5 million Muslims are perceived as having different "needs" from their non-Muslim neighbours. Their interests are often presumed to be about foreign policy rather than domestic issues.

Yet Muslims were no more or less likely to be concerned by the government's decision to invade Iraq, for example, than other citizens of Britain. While first-generation Muslims in Britain may have focused their sights on politics "back home", the younger generations are engaged by social issues here in Britain. "I don't know why they think we need amazingly different things," said Lorraine Hamid, a Whitehall civil servant. There was a strong awareness that voter apathy was a malaise affecting young people everywhere, not just in Muslim homes.

Mayal Timmini, a locum pharmacist, rejected the idea that Muslims vote on faith issues. "I would not be thinking from the point of view of how [politicians] are going to serve the Muslim community, but how are they going to serve the community I live in? Are they going to provide better roads, more jobs? Those are my priorities."

Table 2: What is the impact of the 'war on terror' on British Muslims?

British foreign policy has helped the further integration of Muslims in Britain, despite the vast majority of them being in opposition to it. Muslims have turned their anger into an opportunity to galvanise the community and make their voices heard.

"The 'war on terror' has brought Islam in all its strands, including the political, into the mainstream," said Saqib Mueen, deputy editor of the journal of the Royal United Services Institute. "It has allowed for people to participate in the political process; it has allowed for Muslims to engage in the debate and set the terms of reference."

Muslims were faced with a difficult dilemma in the aftermath of the September 11 attacks on the US, because speaking out led to the question "are you with the terrorists, then?", with the result that Muslims became "bogeymen" and their patriotism was questioned, according to Salma Yaqoob of the Stop the War Coalition.

The government's anti-terrorist laws, including detention without charge or trial, introduced in the wake of 9/11, had been used unfairly against the Muslim community, with an increasing number of stops and searches and arrests — which led to few convictions.

An "unhelpful" climate of fear had been created among Muslims and non-Muslims alike as a result of the new laws, it was agreed. The government's reaction to 9/11 had been a "kneejerk" one, and disproportionate when compared with that of Spain after the real terrorist attack in Madrid this year.

Fatma Dossa, a London-based pharmacist, said there was "no doubt" that Muslims had been targeted by the government. Asad Rehman, a political researcher for George Galloway MP, said: "There's no justification for detention without charge and trial. The key issue is how we respond to this and educate people so that they know their rights."

Asked if there was an onus on Muslims to inform on political or religious groups intent on violence, the group felt this was a "loaded question". They agreed that like any citizen they would condemn what was wrong "whoever is doing it", but one participant, a member of Hizb ut-Tahrir, who did not want to be named, said: "We as the Muslim community need to be the voice of the Muslims abroad, we have failed to do so correctly so far... In my particular view, we have no responsibility to inform on some of the actions of our brothers here supporting what they regard as being just causes abroad."

But Rumeana Jahangir, a media worker, said: "If I found out that somebody was planning to bomb the middle of London I would go and inform because it is *haram* [an act forbidden by the Qur'an]." To which the Hizb ut-Tahrir member said: "I would say to hell with your civic duty." He was interrupted and told that Muslims could not justify killing people.

The rest of the group told him that radical Muslim groups such as his own and that of the extreme preacher Abu Hamza represented "negligible" numbers of Muslims and often made "irrational, illogical comments" that "played into the hands of the media".

> 'The "war on terror" has brought Islam into the mainstream'

"Every pronouncement these groups make sees an increase in attacks on our community," Rehman said.

The Hizb ut-Tahrir member said his party represented a view that was part of the Muslim community. The table then stopped his input, saying: "We are getting distorted by one person."

Table 3: Do you want integration or parallel lives?

Many participants felt they had made headway since the generation of their grandparents, and considered themselves British citizens. But they agreed there were still barriers.

"I think this question is a bit offensive to put the onus on Muslims," said Ayesha Begum. "I mean, we could ask it of any component of British society. Don't we all have to integrate?"

But Hana Al-Hirsi, who works for the Council of Arab-British Understanding, took a different line. "There are communities that do just stick to their own life. I've seen it with my own eyes. The first generation of our parents or our grandparents: some don't speak English although they have been here for 20 or 30 years."

Most participants felt it was an Islamic duty to learn the language and break down barriers. But several regarded themselves as integrated even though they have no non-Muslims among their close friends.

The concern among several participants was that after the struggle to integrate of the first generation, new hurdles are now emerging for those who follow. "Everything around terrorism means we are facing new problems now," Khadija El Shayyal of Young Muslims UK said. "It makes integration more and more difficult, but I have broken barriers my parents weren't able to break."

Reem Maghribi, editor in chief of Sharq, a lifestyle magazine for Arabs, said: "Integration doesn't mean 'become'. It means being involved."

On the issue of Muslim faith schools, there was a wide range of opinions. Ajmal Masroor of the Islamic Society of Britain said he did not see why there needed to be specific Islamic schools, but pointed out that the existing state system had led to highly segregated schools in some areas.

"The only reason we have them is that our education system has failed us miserably," he said. "If the education system was more integrated we would not need separate schools."

Lamin Sesay of the Islamic Community Centre disagreed. "There's no way if I had kids I would have them go near a state school," he said.

"If state schools were better and they adhered to Islamic principles then people would send their children to them — but they don't."

On the question of a distinctive contribution Muslims could make to Britain, the participants agreed that it was the strength of their faith. Ayesha Begum said: "Put God first in everything you do and don't apologise for that. All other values follow, such as honesty and caring. It's the element of morality that is lacking in Britain today."

Raza Kazim said: "In some way we are ambassadors of Islam and that needs to be kept at the forefront."

'Put God first in everything you do and don't apologise for that. All other values follow'

Table 4: Are you satisfied that the leadership of the community reflects your views?

Leadership in the Muslim community will be transformed by an emerging generation, but for now there remains a "capacity gap", with too few resources backing the dynamic leaders of tomorrow, the table agreed.

While British Muslims are drawn from disparate countries and cultures, they share a common identity through their fundamental religious beliefs. Participants agreed that Muslims can, and should, unite on certain "keystone issues", from Iraq and Palestine to religious discrimination.

"On certain keystone issues it's important to show as much unity as possible because that affects your lobbying power with government," said Inayat Bunglawala of the Muslim Council of Britain.

"There is a need to lobby on common issues such as Muslim schools, religious discrimination and incitement to religious hatred, where all Muslims can come together. Because of that unity, we have got results."

"Before we talk on any issue, we have to consult widely," he added. "On Iraq we had to make sure the opinion of the MCB broadly represented the Muslim community as a whole.

"On certain issues, we can articulate forcefully. With other issues we cannot. We can't be in a position where we contribute to divisions."

Muhammad Khan, a youth worker in Birmingham, said it would be unfair to criticise the nascent Muslim leadership too much. "One of the things that's lacking is infrastructure," he said. "Infrastructure enables leadership to work, and that is still emerging and it needs investment, from the community itself and from outside."

While some participants hoped that Muslim businesses would follow their Jewish counterparts in more actively funding their faith, others insisted that leaders could not be artificially created by training schemes and special funds. One of the great strengths of Muslim leadership in Britain, compared with France, was that Muslims had chosen their own leaders and created their own institutions rather than relying on the government to set up "artificial" representative bodies.

The group agreed that more women and young Muslims had to be encouraged to take up leadership positions. According to Azhar Ali, who sits on the Labour party's National Policy Forum, young people are often put off by traditional concepts of leadership in Indian, Pakistani and Bengali Muslim communities.

Several felt that it was not the Muslim faith but western society's treatment of women that was inhibiting their rise into leadership positions. But some women participants were optimistic about a new generation of Muslim leaders who are emerging, particularly from the universities.

Rajnaara Akhtar of the Assembly for the Protection of Hijab said: "Within 10 or 20 years' time we probably won't have this debate. We are still a relatively young community. We are still developing and growing."

'On keystone issues it's important to show as much unity as possible, because that affects your lobbying power'

Table 5: How do the faithful live in a secular society?

"We need to go back to traditional Islam," argued Faraz Yousafzai, a member of Young Citizens in the West Midlands, outlining his vision of taking the original principles of the faith and applying them to a modern context.

"If you apply the principles, that's when you get the right Islam for a particular country."

Sarah Joseph, the editor of emel, a Muslim magazine, said: "Islam is about ethos and morals. It's not about a particular place. So you can have an Islam that draws on British culture and heritage. It's about creating an Islam that is authentically British."

The question of whether a new British Islam was emerging in a secular society dominated the discussion. Other topics, such as the role of the religious leadership, were also considered, but the conversation repeatedly swung back to what a British version of Islam might be.

"We cannot compromise on our religion," said Hasan Abdullah, director of the Islamic Affairs Central Network. "There are certain things that are quite clear, but under pressure we sometimes crumble and try to accommodate them."

On this point most were agreed: there were values central to the faith and these should not be swayed by British norms.

But what those values might be was harder to define. When Asif Dawood, a member of Hizb ut-Tahrir, declared that Islam and democracy were incompatible, there was uproar at the table, with Mr Yousafzai rejecting the idea outright and insisting that the principles of democracy came out of Islam.

There was an assumption, added Sohaib Saeed Bhutta from the Muslim Association of Britain, that there was such a thing as British Islam, when there were differences "within even Glaswegian Islam". A British version of the faith would evolve naturally, he said.

The table discussed whether today's religious leadership was adequate for young Muslims and many felt it was not. Mr Bhutta said: "Imams are failing us." Another participant declared the mosques were no longer relevant.

On the question of whether there are aspects of British culture that the faithful might find offensive, Olga Gora, a convert to Islam, did not feel the question should be directed exclusively at the Muslim community.

"As a woman, I find the position of women immensely disturbing," she said. "Feminism is dead. It's been run over backwards."

There was general agreement that some of the problems Muslims identify in British society are problems for others as well. Islam, said one speaker, did not have a monopoly on morality.

But Anber Raz, a social worker, warned against seeing threats to Islam always from without. "Muslim communities are doing worse things to Islam than anything from the outside," she said, "Racism, sexism, classism — it's all in our own communities. We're doing it to ourselves."

- - - - - - - - - - - - - -
'You can have an Islam that draws on British culture and heritage. It's about creating an Islam that is British'
- - - - - - - - - - - - - -

Table 6: The widespread perception is that Islam discriminates against women. Why is that so?

The body language of the nine women and three men sitting around Table 6 when the question of the hijab was raised was easy to read. One person looked sideways, another sat back in her chair, and a third chuckled. "We're bored of talking about dress codes," said Shatha Khalil, a journalism graduate. "Everyone seems to think the hijab is a symbol of oppression. It's our right. We've chosen it. Get over it."

Others at the table described the headscarf debate as a distraction from more important questions. "We've got all these real issues and we're still talking about the hijab," said Zulfi Bukhari of the Muslim Public Affairs Committee UK.

The women, who dominated the discussion, were clear that they do not feel oppressed by their religion, only by the allegations that they should.

"Why do people believe that Islam discriminates against women?" asked Tahmina Saleem, a press officer for the Muslim Council of Britain.

"There's two common misconceptions. One, we're terrorists, and two, we discriminate against women."

Yasmin Qureshi, Labour's prospective candidate for Brent East, expressed anger at the constant controversy over how Islam treats women. "This perception comes from the media, which doesn't give the correct information," she said. "Some people justify certain actions against women, but that is no different to many other cultures.

"If a Muslim male whose wife is unfaithful kills her, it's perceived as a religious issue."

Many of the women were dismissive of or even defensive towards any allegation that their religion means they are abused or in some way oppressed. The first suggestion that there were any problems for Muslim women's rights came from one of the men on the table, Abdurahman Jafar of the Muslim Council of Britain.

But he emphasised that oppression of Muslim women could not be pinned on religion, or even on their cultural background. "We agree that Islam doesn't discriminate, but men do discriminate, and men control society," he said. "Muslim men seek to justify that oppression under the guise of Islam."

The group agreed that the idea of a ban on headscarfs, as has happened in French schools, was abhorrent. Some suggested that they would prefer to see a ban on the barely dressed pop duo the Cheeky Girls.

Sultanah Parvin, a teacher and member of Hizb ut-Tahrir, picked up on this last point: "Islam is not compatible with western concepts of freedom and choice — they would include the right of women to wear a miniskirt. From an Islamic point of view we don't agree with that." But Ayisha Ali sees this as the challenge of integration. "You might not want to see people in miniskirts, but that's the right of the country we live in, and the law which we have to yield to. It's not up to us to come in and tell them how to live."

> 'We're bored of talking about dress code. Wearing the hijab is our right. Get over it'

Table 7: What are the most pressing problems in your community?

"Our parents came from rural backgrounds and they sometimes find it difficult raising large families in inner-city areas where there are a lot of problems," said Dilowar Hussain Khan of the East London Mosque in Whitechapel.

"They need to be more aware of the issues in this country and what the pitfalls are for their children."

Shebana Khan, a member of the Muslim Council of Britain, pointed out that Muslim families had faced an uphill task from the outset: "Large numbers of Muslims came to this country and settled in industrial towns and then the industries they relied on fell away."

As participants reflected on high levels of deprivation and low educational achievement within the Muslim community, they argued for health and education authorities to work more closely with mosques to provide services.

But mosques and community groups were also encouraged to better reflect their grassroots communities. Imams were urged to play their part in helping people become more outward-looking.

Musab Bora, a community activist from Birmingham, said: "Many of us don't come from the communities we are trying to speak about. Too many institutions develop a gatekeeper mentality and it means the grassroots don't have a voice."

Jamal Al-Shayyal of the Federation of Student Islamic Societies said all of the most pressing problems in the Muslim community related to difficulties faced by families: "I don't think we have had the chance for the family unit to flourish."

For Serena Hussain, a PhD student at Bristol University, the failure of many first-generation parents to negotiate their way around the system has had a particularly damaging effect on the education of their children. "Muslim parents face poverty to a greater extent than other communities," she said. "Parents don't have the experience within the education system and that affects the advice they can give to their children."

Many participants stressed the need for children to have mentors and role models. Khalid Anis of the Islamic Society of Britain said: "One thing that was missing when I was younger was seeing someone who had achieved something great. That is something the Muslim community must provide to raise expectations."

Muslim communities themselves seemed to limit their own aspirations. "I don't see the drive and the ambition that I see in the Indian community and the Jewish community. If you look at our own community you see people who arrive in this country and who have relative prosperity and settle for that."

Samia Rahman, the deputy editor of emel magazine, said even when parents pushed and supported their children, their horizons were limited. Many were happy for their children to enter medicine, but she said: "We need to nurture other professions. Let's get some journalists

> 'We need to nurture other professions. Let's get some journalists into the mainstream media'

into the mainstream media. Then at least we will have a voice."

Arzu Merali, the head of research for the Islamic Human Rights Commission, said stereotyping also held Muslim children back. "We have different people coming to us and saying they want to be doctors, but that their careers teachers have told them to take an accelerated secretarial course instead," she said.

Table 8: How hopeful are you about the future?

The idea that British Muslims might play an equal, valued role in British society by 2010 was dismissed as hopelessly optimistic by the majority of participants.

There was also gloom over the prospects of the "war on terror" — a term with which many felt uneasy — having a peaceful resolution in the foreseeable future.

But there was a feeling that if the Muslim community works together it could — eventually — force changes for the better and, perhaps, one day have more of a positive impact on Muslim countries abroad.

Yusra Khreegi, who has just completed a master's degree in astrophysics, said: "We have to be realistic about what progress can be made. The Muslim community is suffering deprivation in education, economics and integration. That has got to change if we are to play an equal part, and it's not going to happen in just six years."

Sajjad Hoque, a businessman, added: "I'm not hopeful. Until the Muslim community can work together, I don't see how we can move forward."

Romana Majid, an NHS employee, agreed: "We're going to have to work hard as a community to show society that we can make a valuable contribution. Also, the government is failing us."

Ruhul Tarafder, who works for the human rights group The 1990 Trust, added: "We have a very long way to go — look at the racial assaults on Muslim people and the attacks on mosques."

Hooda Sabbah, a voluntary worker, said: "A lot of us feel insecure. We feel like the enemy within."

A note of optimism was sounded by Mohibur Rahman, a special adviser to the Muslim Council of Britain. "Look at the progress we have made — we now have access to halal food and mosques, and Islamic clothes are worn in schools," he said.

International events — US-led wars and the Palestinian conflict, for example — and the government's strengthened legislation to take action against suspected terrorists in the UK were seen as the biggest obstacles to the situation improving by 2010.

The group could not even imagine the "war on terror" ending. "It's a never-ending thing, that's the beauty of it for those leading it," said Abeer Maghribi, a marketing manager. Khreegi added: "The war is about trying to turn people against Muslims."

Representation in the media was also regarded as a big challenge for the Muslim community. "How many Muslims are there in the media?" asked Tabassum Jafri, a pharmacist. "How can we influence a newspaper

'Already some Muslims in France and Spain, for example, look to us. We are too self-deprecating'

like the Sun?"

Adil Khan, a chartered accountant, insisted it could be done: "We are a very talented community with the potential to be very powerful. We have to galvanise the community."

Some members of the group felt the British Muslim community could have a positive impact abroad. Khan said: "Already communities in France and Spain, for example, look to us. Sometimes I think we are too self-deprecating."

But Maghribi said: "It pains me to say it, but we've got to concentrate on the domestic front — we have to leave the international situation for another 20 years."

Reporting team: Audrey Gillan, Steven Morris, Lee Glendinning, Patrick Barkham, Hugh Muir, Helene Mulholland, Polly Curtis, and Faisal al Yafai

Organisations that sent participants include:
The Muslim Council of Britain
The Muslim Association of Britain
The Islamic Society of Britain
Muslim News
Islamic Forum Europe
Forum Against Islamophobia and Racism
Federation of Student Islamic Societies
Islamic Affairs Central Network
Hizb ut-Tahrir
Al-Hasaniya Moroccan Women's Centre
The Islamic Foundation
The Assembly for the Protection of the Hijab
The Muslim Public Affairs Committee UK
The London Muslim Centre
The Islamic Human Rights Commission
Young Muslims UK
The Stop the War Coalition

How to face up to perceptions — and frame the right questions
Reported by Audrey Gillan

'Even though you are saying you are asking us as Muslims, why are you not asking the same question of others?'

The British Muslim community is ahead of any other Muslim community in Europe and has a far more sophisticated understanding of its place in society, but it should stop being so defensive, according to Tariq Ramadan, a Geneva-based author and academic who is one of the most revered Muslim scholars in the world.

The answers found by Muslims in Britain and their counterparts in France to current problems would provide solutions for other Muslims elsewhere in the world, he believes.

Ramadan, who is listed as one of Time magazine's Top 100 thinkers because of his desire to shape an independent European Islam — and who recently had his working visa revoked by the US — was the main focus of attention in a panel of five invited guests who addressed the gathering of young Muslims.

He told them to "get rid of the defensive attitude; it is important that, as Muslims, we are not put on the defensive."

There was a problem of perception they had to tackle head on when being asked questions that they considered uncomfortable or offensive, such as: "Do you want to integrate?" or "How would you describe your identity?"

"The point is that even though you are saying you are asking us as Muslims, why are you not asking the same question of others?

"Just because they are not asking others does not mean that the question is not legitimate. You cannot get rid of perceptions by saying that your question is wrong. It's like saying to someone who says to you, 'I am scared, I feel that you are a threat to this society,' and you say, 'No, it's not good to be scared'.

"If I am scared, I am scared. Now try to help me to put it in another way; we need to go beyond this perception."

The way forward was to be more precise in dealing with such questions, to begin to frame the questions themselves. To do so, Muslims had to master the terminology and have a methodology.

"I really think that this is our contribution to our discussion in this society when we think about multiculturalism, identity, integration. A better discourse coming from Muslims requires mastering the terminology."

Muslims had to deal not only with angry feelings about their religion, but make points about their social problems, economic problems and political involvement, and should work towards the recognition that "to be critical towards the British government does not mean that you are not loyal to the government. In fact it is the opposite; constructive criticism means that I am really British."

Humera Khan, a founder of the Muslim women's An-Nisa Society, disagreed, saying she had been disappointed by the questions: "These are Guardian journalists' and readers' idiosyncrasies we are trying to come to terms with."

Trevor Phillips, who chairs the Commission for Racial Equality, said such questions should not be seen as attacks but as "opportunities". Every other minority community in the UK could learn lessons from Muslims, he added, because of how it had managed to unite and develop a strong lobby in the MCB.

Tim Winter, fellow of Wolfson College, Cambridge, and imam of Cambridge mosque, said the majority of the British public had no idea such questions were even being raised and argued over, nor that on most of the key issues there was nothing resembling a consensus among Muslims.

"We are sympathetic to leftwing perceptions in terms of foreign policy, but our instincts tend to be with the right in domestic politics," Winter said.

"Naturally, we are horrified by what's happening in Iraq and the West Bank in the same way that it horrifies the secular left, but on domestic policy we recoil when we are told about new abortion legislation or same-sex marriages and the other domestic issues of the day.

"That makes it really difficult for us to see wholeheartedly where Muslims belong in the established political spectrum in this country.

"It is not something I have a solution to and it's not going to be resolved by being in a Liberal Democrat grey area. It probably means that people of passionate, religious conviction are going to be at one remove from the established language and logic of political discussion.

"We are always going to be coming at this from a slightly eccentric angle."

Not surprisingly, the greatest anger was directed at the government. Panelist Fiona Mactaggart, a minister at the Home Office, was roundly booed when she declared that Muslims were not victims of foreign policy or of the government's anti-terrorism laws, introduced in the wake of the September 11 attacks, which have led to detentions of Muslims without charge and trial.

"We have leading Muslims on the stop and search action team that we have established to try to make sure that, if there is disproportionality in the way this legislation works, which there might be, then it is justified by evidence," she said. "And if it isn't justified by evidence, we will end it."

But the audience greeted her comments with derision and refused to accept that the government had promoted the interests of Muslims on issues such as new legislation on incitement to religious hatred.

... And why we urgently need new answers

Sarfraz Manzoor

'To actually hear some of the experiences of British Muslims since 9/11 made for grim listening'

The walls of the university hall were plastered with signs that read "Being Muslim and British" with an arrow pointing forwards. The arrows directed us to a large hall where, for the next three hours, we heard young British Muslims discuss among themselves the compatibilities and contradictions of being British and Muslim.

By the end of the evening I left less certain which direction the signs were pointing.

The event was an intriguing blend of speed dating and dinner party; eight tables of impassioned conversation between strangers, with me floating from table to table, eavesdropping in when the discussions threatened to get interesting. It was impossible not to feel energised to see so many people all talking eloquently and fluently; what was disappointing was what so many of them were saying.

A study published on the same night as the gathering, by the Open Society Institute, revealed the depth of estrangement between British Muslims and their country. One-third of those surveyed said they had been discriminated against at British airports because of their religion; the number of Asians stopped and searched under the Terrorism Act rose 302% between 2001 and 2003, and 80% said they had experienced Islamophobia.

It has become a commonplace to note that British Muslims, like Muslims everywhere, have felt victimised since September 11 2001. To actually hear some of the experiences made for grim listening, and perhaps it is not surprising that when a community feels embattled, it becomes defensive.

If there was one overpowering sensation on the night it was awareness of that defensiveness; the sound of a community hardened by its experience. "You can never be 100% British," argued one woman, who looked as though she might be in a girl band. Hearing such comments (one man said "I wouldn't want my daughter to go through what I went through") made it seem to many in the hall as though there had been precious little progress since the experiences their parents went through in the 60s and 70s.

The purpose of the gathering was to address some specific questions, but what came through loudly for me was the reluctance of many to actually address them. Rather than grapple with some of the genuine concerns the rest of the country has about Islam, it was easier to argue semantics than substance. What do you mean by integration? What do you mean by identity? What do you mean by British? It seemed easier to squabble over definitions.

Most of the opinions felt rehearsed; what was surprising was that it was impossible to gauge from appearance what viewpoint was about to be expressed. And for every young man who argued that being British was a territorial identity there were others who said it was about accepting cultural values.

In the end, however, the settled conclusions of the groups were less nuanced. There were the usual complaints against the portrayal of Muslims in the media and the British government's foreign policy, and a general grumble that anyone even dared to ask about the loyalty and commitment of British Muslims to their country. This reluctance to be self-critical may be partly a result of feeling embattled and not wanting to wash dirty laundry in front of others, but I think it is also owing to a failure of creative thinking from British Muslims. Put simply, there is a tendency to want to have the cultural cake and eat it too: to say yes we are different and no we are not different at the same time.

The fact is that many people in the UK and elsewhere have concerns about British Muslims, and to just argue that they are misguided will neither reassure them nor provide a route towards conciliation.

Too many of the self-proclaimed leaders among British Muslims seem more keen on furthering other agendas of politics, self-interest and self-promotion than in chiselling away at the tough questions. That requires a more rigorous degree of thinking and, thankfully, there were some signs of it in the hall. There was the woman who said: "There is racism and sexism in our community; we do it to ourselves"; and the man who added that "Islam does not have a monopoly on morality"; and the many participants who said people are entitled to more than one identity.

The parents of the group who gathered in that hall could never have attended such a meeting; that such a forum can now take place is a sign of progress. These young men and women are eloquent and not short of confidence. The challenge they, and all British Muslims, face is to not withdraw into defensiveness or a predictable reheating of old complaints, but instead to think deeper and harder about some of the issues that were discussed and to have the courage to offer some new answers.